Holy Humor

Holy Humor

A Book of Inspirational Wit and Cartoons

CAL AND ROSE SAMRA

Guideposts®

CARMEL • NEW YORK 10512

This Guideposts edition is published by special arrangement with MasterMedia Limited.

ISBN 1-57101-057-2

Designed by Michael Woyton
Manufactured in the United States of America

To Jesus,
whose overflowing joy,
humor, love and mercy
made this book possible.

"Angels can fly because they take themselves lightly. Never forget that Satan fell by force of gravity."
—G.K. Chesterton

"God laughs because He knows more than we do. God has sharper vision."
—Miriam Pollard

"Communion is strength; solitude is weakness. Alone, the fine old beech yields to the blast and lies prone on the meadow. In the forest, supporting each other, the trees laugh at the hurricane."
—Charles Spurgeon

Contents

$\mathscr{A}$cknowledgments

Humor, like love, crosses denominational lines. In 1994, the mainline Associated Church Press, the Catholic Press Association, and the Evangelical Press Association finally agreed on one thing: *The Joyful Noiseletter* is an award-winning laugher. The monthly newsletter of the interdenominational Fellowship of Merry Christians won awards of excellence for newsletters from all three religious press associations.

It was a first. *JN* is the only publication which is a member of all three religious press associations. There are those who might even suggest it is a miracle to get that kind of consensus from judges with such divergent views.

* The Associated Church Press judges wrote: *"This outstanding newsletter does what it's supposed to do — it makes you laugh. Great fun! A joy to read! Useful to church newsletter editors, particularly."*

* The Catholic Press Association judges wrote: *"Here is humor that is relevant, comical but free of profanity and blasphemy so blatantly featured in the modern media. Impressive graphics and snappy writing fill this newsletter with life and wisdom."*

* The Evangelical Press Association judges wrote: *"Chock-full of digestible tidbits. Highly readable and lots of fun. What a great publication!"*

These awards belong to the many gifted members of the Fellowship of Merry Christians — clean comedians, humorists, cartoonists, clowns, toastmasters, clergy, health professionals, and lay people of all denominations — who have generously contributed holy humor and good cheer to *The Joyful Noiseletter* for the past 10 years.

"A church that lacks humor lacks reality and closeness to its members," says cartoonist Bil Keane, creator of *The Family Circus*, America's beloved No. 1 cartoon family. Bil is a charter member of the fellowship and has been one of its guiding lights from its beginnings. We thank Bil especially for his generosity in sharing so much of the holy humor in *The Family Circus* with *JN*.

We are most grateful, too, to another charter member, cartoonist Ed Sullivan, a brilliant satirist with a large heart, who has contributed many of his "Beyond the Stained Glass" cartoons to this book.

JN also has been blessed with the wit and wisdom of talented cartoonists like Johnny Hart (*B.C.*), Bob Thaves (*Frank & Ernest*), Harley Schwadron, Jonny Hawkins, Dennis Daniel (*Brother Blooper*), Goddard Sherman, Ed Koehler, Doc Goodwin (*Phillip's Flock*), Wendell W. Simons, Steve Phelps, Dik Lapine, Karl R. Kraft, M. Larry Zanco, Dick Hafer, Larry M. White, Al Johns of *Cartoons by Johns*, and the late Sandy Dean.

We are also most grateful for the rib-tickling contributions of our consulting editors and members. These include many humorists: Liz Curtis Higgs, Hall of Fame broadcaster Joe Garagiola, Sr. Mary Christelle Macaluso ("The Fun Nun"), Ron Birk (a Lutheran Texas goat rancher), George and Peggy Goldtrap, Chaplain Cy Eberhart (who does a marvelous imitation of Will Rogers), Edward R. Walsh (an authority on Will Rogers), Tom Mullen (a Quaker humorist who sounds like Will Rogers), Ardith Talbot (a Quaker "hat humorist"), Dr. Donald L. Cooper (Oklahoma State University team physician and Reagan appointee to the President's Council on Physical Fitness and Sports), humorist-magician Doyne Michie (who has a "ministry of laughter" to hospitals); Lois Donahue; Cliff Thomas, R.Ph. ("The Philosophical Pharmacist" who charges for prescriptions but gives out his jokes free), Dr. Dale L. Anderson (the physician-humorist who shows you how to "conduct your way to greater health and happiness"), Mike Tighe, Karyn Buxman, RN (an authority on Mark Twain and therapeutic humor), satirist David R. Francoeur (creator of the "Balmy Clergy Supply" ads for Christmas gifts for clergy), humor historian Paul Thigpen, and epigrammatist Denny Brake.

Special thanks to jokesters Pastor Dennis R. Fakes and to Msgr. Arthur J. Tonne (who, at the age of 91, is working on

his ninth volume of *Jokes Priests Can Tell* books), and to Jim
Reed for his collection of clergy golf jokes from his book, *The
Funny Side of Golf.* We are also grateful to humor theologians
Conrad Hyers, Rev. Lee van Rensburg, Fr. Tom Walsh,
Sherwood Eliot Wirt (a long-time associate of Billy Graham,
who, at the age of 85, wrote a splendid book, *The Book of Joy*),
and Terry R. Lindvall (author of a delightful soon-to-be-
published book, *Surprised by Laughter: The Comic World of
C.S. Lewis,* and a scholar who is also an authority on G. K.
Chesterton).

JN also has been blessed by some very funny contributions
from comedians like Merrilyn Belgum ("The World's
Funniest Old Lady"), Tommy DiNardo, Adam Christing
(founder of the Clean Comedians), Steve Allen, Messianic
Jewish comedians Steve Feldman and Burt Rosenberg, and
Pastor Paul Lintern (who started "Saturday Night Alive"
shows at his Lutheran church).

Great gratitude also must go to the many clowns and
"holy fools" who are members of the Fellowship: Don
("Ski") and Ruby ("Tah Dah!") Berkoski (whose Smiles
Unlimited clown ministry to hospitals and prisons was
featured in a *Guideposts* Easter issue), Karen Wilson Fox
(who launched a program that sent volunteers dressed as
Raggedy Ann and Raggedy Andy into hospitals to visit and
cheer up patients — another story that was featured in
Guideposts), Ed and Marji Elzey ("Marji and Roma," who
have a charming mime-music ministry), John Lang, John and
Therese Boucher, Donna ("M.T. Pockets") Wilinski, and
Hunter ("Patch") Adams, M.D. (the "clown-prince of
physicians" who founded the Gesundheit Institute in
Arlington, VA, after a bout with depression).

Thanks, too, to humor librarians Connie Soth and Mary
Margaret Jordan; playshop leaders Gina Bridgeman and Sr.
Monique Rysavy, SSND, columnist Dolores Curran, Dr. Rich
Bimler (the effervescent president of Wheat Ridge
Ministries), Andy Fisher (senior writer for *The Today Show*),
Fr. Norman J. Muckerman, CSSR (former editor of *Liguorian*
magazine), Jean Spencer, Fr. John Catoir (director of the

Christophers), Dr. Winslow Fox, Fr. Brian Cavanaugh, William W. Willimon, Fr. Ronald P. Lengwin, Barbara Shlemon Ryan, Episcopal Bishop Arthur Vogel, Fr. Martin Clarke, OFM, Cap, Fr. Martin Wolter, OFM, Leslie M. Gibson, RN (who instituted comedy carts for patients at Morton Plant Hospital in Florida), Lou Jacquet (associate editor of the *Catholic Exponent* in Youngstown, OH), Navy Lt. James M.T. Connolly, aka "Chaplain Bubbles" (aboard the U.S.S. Enterprise) and Catherine Hall and Charles J. Milazzo for their one-liners.

We are especially grateful to artist Jack Jewell for his donation of his painting "The Risen Christ by the Sea" to the Fellowship.

We also salute *JN's* "celestial consulting editors," who were consulting editors to *JN* before going to their joyful Lord: Baptist Pastor Tal D. Bonham (author of several *Treasury of Clean Jokes* books); George W. Cornell (long-time religion writer for the Associated Press), cartoonist Sandy Dean, Fr. George DePrizio, CSC, Pastor Jakob Jonsson, Dom Jean Leclercq, Archbishop John L. May of St. Louis (who always ended his weekly column in his diocesan newspaper with a joke), Malcolm Muggeridge, and Rev. Canon Alfred W. Price (the witty Episcopal warden of the Order of St. Luke the Physician.)

Fr. DePrizio, a chaplain at Cabrini Medical Center in New York City and a retreat director, was the author of *Are You Laughing with Me, Jesus?* He lived to the age of 81.

The great English humorist Malcolm Muggeridge, the former editor of *Punch* who later became a convert to Christianity, joined *JN's* board of consulting editors a couple of years before his death at the ripe old age of 87.

In his last book, *Confessions of a 20th-Century Pilgrim*, "St. Mugg" wrote: "The assumption that a sense of humour and a Christian faith are incompatible is totally mistaken. In point of fact, the writers of the great classics of humor — like Cervantes, Swift, Gogal — have all been deeply religious...

"There is a close connection between clowns and mystics... Laughter, indeed, is God's therapy; He planted the steeples and the gargoyles, gave us clowns as well as saints, in order that we might understand that at the heart of our mortal existence, there lies a mystery, at once unutterably beautiful and hilariously funny."

Pastor Jakob Jonsson, a Lutheran minister in the Icelandic Church, is another *JN* consulting editor who lived to an old age. (The number of humorists who live to a ripe old age suggests that there may well be a relationship between a sense of humor and longevity.) Pastor Jonsson was the author of a little-known but fascinating book called *Humor and Irony in the New Testament, Illustrated by Parallels in the Talmud and Midrash*, published in English in 1965 by E.J. Brill, Leiden, The Netherlands.

Jonsson made an extensive study of the Jewish roots of Christian humor, delving into "the fascinating world of rabbinic literature," the Old Testament, and the New Testament. He concluded that "the authors of the New Testament were influenced by rabbinic humour and the prophetic irony of the Old Testament."

Jonsson observed, "The Jewish rabbis were aware that paradox, sympathetic irony, and humour can be effective teaching methods. This helps us to a better understanding of how the Rabbi Jesus taught. Jesus also used humour to teach."

Catholic theologian Dom Jean Leclercq of Luxembourg, who died at the age of 83, wrote an article titled "In Praise of Laughter" for one of *JN's* first issues, observing, "The Desert Fathers of the early church were renowned for their humor, and regarded hilarity as both a gift of the Holy Spirit and a virtue to acquire, to hold onto, and to preach about."

We wish to thank Broadman & Holman Publishers of Nashville, TN, for permission to reprint some of our favorite jokes from Tal D. Bonham's book, *The Treasury of Clean Church Jokes*, available from the FMC catalog and Christian bookstores; Msgr. Arthur Tonne for permission to reprint some of our favorite jokes from his books *Jokes Priests Can Tell*; and Alba House of Staten Island, NY, for permission to reprint some of the cartoons from Ed Sullivan's book, *A Gift of Laughter.* (All of these books are available from the FMC catalog.)

We are especially grateful for the joy and humor which we have received from our children, Luke Samra, Paul Samra, Matt Samra and his wife, Becky, and from the McBride and Samra families.

Thousands of people from the entire theological and political spectrum — from comedian Steve Allen in Van Nuys, CA, to Dr. Terry R. Lindvall, president of Regent University in Virginia Beach, VA — have sent *The Joyful Noiseletter* jokes, funny stories, spoonerisms, bulletin bloopers, out-of-the-mouths-of-babes quotes, inspirational humor, prayers and uplifting Scripture passages.

We thank all of these wonderful people, and we thank God for the joy and laughter they have brought into our lives and the lives of thousands of others.

> "Be not forgetful to entertain strangers; for thereby some have entertained angels unawares."
> —Hebrews 13:2

$\mathcal{J}$ntroduction

In all humility,
The World's Greatest Collection
of Inspirational Humor

"Jesters do often prove prophets," Shakespeare wrote. Many Christians do not know that Christianity has a rich tradition of humor, wit, good cheer, joy and celebration going back to its beginnings.

Just as many health professionals, influenced by Norman Cousins' insightful book *The Anatomy of an Illness*, are now rediscovering the healing power of humor and laughter, many churches of all denominations are also rediscovering the healing power of Christian joy and humor.

An old Eastern church tradition says that Lazarus laughed heartily for years after Jesus raised him from the dead. That is why Lazarus' home in Bethany, the Holy Land, is called "The House of Laughter."

Ten years ago, a group of Christian humorists, comedians, jokesters, cartoonists, and clowns organized a "House of Laughter" — the Fellowship of Merry Christians. The Fellowship and its monthly newsletter, *The Joyful Noiseletter*, celebrates our 10th anniversary in 1996.

The first issue of *JN* appeared on April Fools' Day, 1986, with the suggestion that readers try to follow the Apostle Paul's admonition to be "fools for Christ's sake."

Now, in celebration of the Fellowship's 10th anniversary, we, the editors and founders of *The Joyful Noiseletter*, have brought together many of the best and the funniest of *JN's* cartoons, jokes, anecdotes, bulletin bloopers, and one-liners in this book. The chapters in this book are arranged in calendar-year order, the same way that churches and other subscribers are accustomed to receiving *The Joyful Noiseletter.*

The idea for the Fellowship of Merry Christians developed from a 1985 book written by Cal Samra (then a newspaper reporter) and published by Harper & Row: *The Joyful Christ: The Healing Power of Humor.* (The book describes Cal's pilgrimage from depression and despair to new life in the joyful Christ. In the book, Cal maintains that Jesus was a joyful Spirit when He walked this earth and after His resurrection, and that He used humor in His healing ministry.)

After the book was published, many pastors and lay people of all denominations wrote to the author and suggested the formation of an organization and a newsletter that would continue to focus on the joy and humor in the Christian life. Everyone dumps heavy stuff on the clergy, they said, and what was needed was an interdenominational publication to provide them with clean jokes, cartoons, and upbeat anecdotes to use in their sermons and reprint in their church newsletters.

Thus were born FMC and *JN*. On *JN's* masthead is this message: "Our modest aim is to recapture the spirit of joy, humor, unity, and healing power of the early Christians. We try to be merry more than twice a year."

Through the years, thousands of pastors and church newsletter editors have joined the Fellowship and used and reprinted the inspirational humor in *The Joyful Noiseletter.* But many other people hungry for inspirational humor have also joined the Fellowship: health professionals and counselors desiring to add a humorous dimension to their practices; youth ministers, Sunday school and religious education teachers; toastmasters and speakers; persons involved in humor and clown ministries; church and seminary librarians; police officers and prisoners; patients struggling against illness; and people of other faiths who enjoy sharing good humor and healing laughter.

These people all believe that it is possible to be reverent and moral and still have fun. *JN's* focus has been on the things that unite Christians, not on the things that divide them.

The late George Cornell, the long-time religion writer for the Associated Press, described *JN's* style as follows: "In dispensing 'holy humor, '*The Joyful Noiseletter* adheres to certain standards for it, such as that it exalts the lowly and deflates the proud, that it cheers people rather than wounds, that it honors moral values rather than mocks them."

The Fellowship has pioneered the use of holy humor as a bridge-building, peace-making, healing, and evangelistic tool.

As it has grown, the Fellowship has become *the* resource center for books, audio and video cassettes, and prints which focus on the joy, hu mor, celebration, and healing power in the Christian faith. A bibliography of our catalog offerings is available at the back of this book. Many of the contributors to this book are authors and speakers whose humor books and cassettes are available in the FMC catalog.

Jesus loves a good party, as He clearly demonstrated when He performed His first miracle at a wedding reception in Cana, and as He again clearly demonstrated in His parable of the Prodigal Son.

The Fellowship also pioneered the use of "playshops" to tickle congregations to life. The Fellowship has co-sponsored playshops and retreats with churches, retreat centers, and hospitals to help persons seeking the gift of a sense of humor to bring more joy into their lives. Participants are encouraged to take God seriously, but themselves less seriously.

FMC playshops are parties celebrating the joyful, triumphant, Risen Christ.

The Fellowship published a *Playshop Guidebook* which contains a model program for a unique, modestly priced, one-day playshop. The *Playshop Guidebook* also contains photographs and biographical sketches of 34 gifted Christian humorists who are available as playshop leaders.

The Fellowship also has become widely known for its annual celebration in April of "Holy Humor Month," which has been listed annually in *Chase's Calendar of Events* since 1988.

"Holy Humor Month" is an extended celebration of the resurrection of Jesus. The Fellowship encourages Christians to be "fools for Christ's sake" (1 Cor. 4:10) on April Fools' Day, following an ancient Christian tradition of "holy fools." The Fellowship also encourages churches and prayer groups to celebrate "The Easter Laugh" — God's last laugh on the devil when He raised Jesus from the dead — with Easter Monday and Bright Sunday (the Sunday after Easter) festivities.

The Fellowship is aiming to resurrect a very old Christian custom — Easter Monday parties — in celebration of Jesus' resurrection. Easter Monday traditionally was celebrated as a "Day of Joy and Laughter" in Catholic, Orthodox, and Protestant countries.

In recent years, Holy Humor Month has been observed ingeniously, imaginatively, and humorously by a variety of churches and prayer groups, and they've had a lot of fun doing it. (See Chapter 4.) We hope that Holy Humor Month activities will help shore up belief in Jesus' resurrection, which has been increasingly under attack.

At Christmas time, 1994, the Fellowship also announced its first annual Scrooge Award and its first annual True Spirit of Christmas Present Award.

The Fellowship's Scrooge Award is given annually "to the organization or group whose humbug most insistently dampens the Spirit of Christmas at Christmas time." The True Spirit of Christmas Present Award is given annually "to the person or organization who best exemplifies the True Spirit of Christmas Present." (See Chapter 12 for the 1994 and 1995 award winners.)

For the record, we value the healing gift of tears as well as the healing gift of laughter. Both gifts are from God. Most gratifying of all are the thousands of letters and calls we have received from people of all denominations, saying that

JN, or a book or cassette offered in the FMC catalog, or an FMC playshop have lifted their spirits, brought them healing laughter, helped them through a depression or an illness, or eased the pain of loss. Holy humor is clearly an ally of clergy, health professionals, and lay people in the battle against human suffering, depression, and illness, and it should be taken seriously.

Holy humor also is a powerful peace-making and bridge-building tool that can be used to defuse anger and hatred, reduce tensions, and resolve conflicts.

It has always intrigued us that the word "humor" and the word "humility" both have the same root, deriving from the Latin word *"humus,"* meaning "of the earth." Humor reminds us of our fragility, our earthiness, our dustiness, our propensity to mess things up even when we have the best of intentions, our powerlessness apart from God. Humor shows each of us how far we have fallen short of the glory of God.

In all humility, we think that this book is "The World's Greatest Collection of Inspirational Humor." We hope it will open the reader's eyes to how many follies, as well as virtues, we share in common in all denominations.

On the very eve of His crucifixion, Jesus said to His disciples: "These things I have spoken to you that my *joy* may be in you, and your *joy* may be full." (John 15:11) The Man knows He's about to be nailed to a cross, and He's talking about *joy*!

Let us remember that He told us to "be of good cheer." Enjoy!

—Cal and Rose Samra
Editors

~ Chapter 1 ~
January

Happy New Year!
'Keep runnin' and don't look back'

THE FAMILY CIRCUS

"Yesterday's the past, tomorrow's
the future, but today is a *gift*. That's
why it's called the *present*."

The Apostle Paul told the Philippians: "Forgetting what is behind and straining toward what is ahead, I press on toward the goal to win the prize..." The great philosopher Satchel Paige, who according to some probably knew Paul, may have been only paraphrasing him when he said: "Keep runnin' and don't look back, because somebody might be gainin' on you."

"Satchel, who pitched in the Major Leagues at the age of 48, used to say, 'How old would you be if you didn't know how old you are?' I know 20-year-old guys with 90-year-old minds, and 90-year-old guys with 20-year-old minds."
—Joe Garagiola
It's Anybody's Ballgame

"The One whose throne is in heaven sits laughing."
—Psalm 2:4

"In Nigeria, the name of God is 'Father of Laughter.' "
—Joseph R. Veneroso
Maryknoll magazine

"Once the hand is laid to the plow, no one who looks back is fit for the kingdom of God."
—Jesus Christ
(Luke 9:62)

"I've always felt that people are better off looking ahead than looking back. Jack Benny felt the same way. 'The heck with the past,' he used to say."
—George Burns at 95

Without informing his wife, an Anglican priest invited his bishop to stay overnight at his home after a confirmation. Before supper, the bishop was walking down a dimly-lit corridor in the priest's home. The priest's wife, coming up from behind, mistook the bishop for her husband and gave him a clout over the ear. "That'll teach you to ask the bishop to stay when we've got nothing in the house," she snapped.

—*The Anglican Digest*

"My neighbor, the Rev. H.J. Dick, pastor of Emmaus Mennonite Church near Whitewater, KS, came to the end of a very heavy day at the New Year's Eve midnight service. Getting his tongue tangled, he announced: 'Let us now stand and sing, Another Dear Is Yawning.' "

—Rev. Louis G. Poppe
Blue Springs, MO

FMC member Pastor Dave Buuck of Joy Lutheran Church, Cambridge, MN, made the following New Year's resolution: "I resolve to turn my microphone off when I go out of the chancel to blow my nose during a church service."

FMC member Karl M. Harsney of Bath, PA, passes on this story, which he heard Lutheran Pastor Peter Unks tell in a sermon:

A paramedic was asked on a local TV

"Bring some zest into your life in the New Year! Make a friend; fall in love; paint a picture, write a poem, express your inner self; speak with a sweet tongue and be slow to anger; give a children's party; take ballroom dancing lessons ..."

© 1994 Ed Sullivan

talk-show program: "What was your most unusual and challenging 911 call?"

"Recently, we got a call from that big white church at 11th and Walnut," the paramedic said. "A frantic usher was very concerned that during the sermon an elderly man passed out in a pew and appeared to be dead. The usher could find no pulse and there was no noticeable breathing."

"What was so unusual and demanding about this particular call?" the interviewer asked.

"Well," the paramedic said, "we carried out four guys before we found the one who was dead."

A cardinal was approached one day in the cathedral by a very excited young priest. "Your Eminence," the priest cried, "a woman claims to have seen a vision of the Savior in the chapel. What should we do?"

"Look busy," the cardinal said. "Look busy."
—Sophia Bar

A confirmation student was asked to list the Ten Commandments in any order. He wrote: "3, 6, 1, 8, 4, 5, 9, 2, 10, 7."
—*The Lutheran*

Eleventh commandment: "Thou shalt not committee."
—Baptist Pastor Tal Bonham

"Never clutch the past so tightly that it leaves your arms unable to embrace the present. Happy New Year!"
—St. Rocco's Church newsletter
Martins Creek, PA

"In Rome many people maintain the custom of throwing something out the window on New Year's Eve. What a relief to get rid of every old resentment, every old fear, old prejudices, old notions, old ways of doing things."
—Dr. Norman Vincent Peale

The place to be happy is here;
The time to be happy is now;
The way to be happy is to make others so.
　　　　　—via Pastor John J. Walker
　　　　　First Christian Church
　　　　　Post, TX

Tony Lloyd, a Seventh-Day Adventist student at Walla Walla College in WA, made the following New Year's resolution: "I resolve, no matter what happens, to look for the best and try to keep a smile on my face."

Received in the morning mail:
And Jesus said, "Who do you say I am?"
And they answered: "You are the eschatological manifestation of the ground of our being, the kerygma in which we found the ultimate meaning of our interpersonal relationship."
And Jesus said, "What?"

"Here I am, Lord. A New Year. A fresh awakening. Ready to serve you with all my strength. Ready to wrestle with Satan. Ready to serve others and fight for right. Ready to win the lottery..."

© 1992 Ed Sullivan

And God said:
"My name is not *I Was.*
"My name is not *I Will Be.*
"My name is *I Am.*"
　　　　　—via Sue Lytwyn
　　　　　Kalamazoo, MI

A keynote speaker at a convention of priests came to the dais, shuffled his notes, scanned his audience, and said, thoughtfully:

"Where to begin? Where to begin?"
A voice in the crowd yelled: "As close to the end as possible!"
—Fr. Norman J. Muckerman, CSSR
Liguori, MO

Woman to pastor: "You don't know how much your sermons have meant to my husband since he lost his mind."
—Tal Bonham

"I talked to a fellow not long ago who had been preaching in Kentucky. I asked where he'd been preaching. He said in Hazard, KY. That's way back in the Appalachians, you know. He said it was so far back in the woods that even the Episcopalians were handling snakes."
—George Goldtrap
Madison, TN

After Dr. Lloyd John Ogilvie, senior pastor of the First Presbyterian Church of Hollywood, CA, was elected U.S. Senate Chaplain in 1994, he wrote to the editor of *JN* saying he appreciated the crucial ministry to bring joy and good cheer into the lives of Christians. Dr. Ogilvie will appreciate this story:

A small boy, visiting the U.S. Senate with his father, asked him: "What does the Chaplain of Congress do?"
"He stands up, looks at the Congress, and prays for the country," the father answered.

"About all I can say about the United States Senate is that it opens with a prayer, and closes with an investigation."
—Will Rogers

"Religion will disappear."
—Karl Marx
"Karl Marx has disappeared."
—God

"Mirth is God's medicine. Everybody ought to bathe in it. Grim care, moroseness, anxiety — all this rust of life — ought to be scoured off by the oil of mirth."
—Henry Ward Beecher

"A good laugh heals a lot of hurts."
—Madeleine L'Engle

"PLEASE HELP ME, FATHER,' FRED WATCHES FOOTBALL ON TV ALL DAY LONG AND I CAN'T GET HIM TO STOP..."

"SEND HIM OVER AND WE'LL TALK."

© 1995 Ed Sullivan

"People go to a football game today and shout their heads off, or go to a circus and cheer act after act. They become enthusiastic about everything conceivable, but when it comes to spiritual matters they think we are supposed to become sober and wear black, and never have a good time or enjoy a religious event."
—Billy Graham

"I've found that prayers work best when you have big players."
—Knute Rockne

"Then they gave their newborn the name revered in all the territory — 'Coach.' "
—Pastor Denny Brake
Raleigh, NC

He's an hour and a half early
For the football games,
And the last one
From the dressing room door.
He's oblivious to pain,
Or even to rain
When it's the tenth
And still tied is the score.
He's glued to the tube
When the sudden-death match
Takes another
Two holes for the win.
And it matters not
If the last second shot
Makes a third overtime
Go beyond ten.
But come Sunday morn,
As he sits in the pew,
This sports-loving spouse
Very soon
Begins to get nervous
If the one-hour service
Finds the pastor preaching
A minute past noon.

—Dona Maddux Cooper
Stillwater, OK

The congregation of the First Methodist Church of Houston, TX, presented its distinguished pastor, Dr. Charles Allen, with a new color television set on an anniversary Sunday. That afternoon, Dr. Allen settled in his easy chair to watch the Raiders play the Cowboys.

Mrs. Allen spoke gently to her husband, suggesting that perhaps the congregation did not present them with the new set for watching football on the Lord's Day.

"Don't think a thing about it, dear," said Dr. Allen. "Just leave it where it is; Billy Graham will be coming on any minute now."
—Sherwood Eliot Wirt
The Book of Joy

The Most Rev. Robert Runcie, retired Archbishop of Canterbury, wrote in his book, *Seasons of the Spirit*, that he once got on a train in England and discovered that all of the other passengers in the car were patients at a mental institution being taken on an excursion.

A mental hospital attendant was counting the patients to be sure that they were all there: "One, two, three, four, five…" When he came to Runcie, he said, "Who are you?"

Taking a cue from John Madden, Pastor Mel diagrams the morning offering for the ushers.
© 1995 Steve Phelps

"I am the Archbishop of Canterbury," Runcie replied.

The attendant smiled and, pointing to him, continued counting, "…six, seven, eight…"
—via Rev. Stuart A. Schlegel
Los Gatos, CA

A fine preacher named Tweedle
Said as he refused a degree,
It's tough enough being Tweedle,
Without being Tweedle, D.D.
—James C. Hefley
Way Back in the 'Korn' Fields

Eager to improve his sermons, a young pastor bought a tape recorder and recorded one of his Sunday morning services. After dinner, he put the cassette in the recorder, sat on the sofa, and listened to the tape.

The opening prayer, scripture readings, and hymns came forth nicely. Then came the sermon.

When he awoke some time later, the choir was singing the closing hymn.

—Msgr. Arthur Tonne
Jokes Priests Can Tell

"We are all here for a spell. Get all the good laughs you can."

—Will Rogers

At an FMC playshop, Archbishop John L. May of St. Louis told this story:

"Down in Southern Missouri, we have the Ozarks and the people down there don't know much about Catholics. A priest's car stalled on a back road, and he went to a small house to find help. The nice couple there said they had never met anyone with a collar on backwards."

The priest said, "Yeah, but how come you have a picture of the pope on the wall?"

"Where?" they asked. The priest pointed to a picture on the wall. It was a picture of Pope Pius XII, a former pope who wore glasses.

"Who's that?" they asked.

"The pope," the priest said.

"Oh, my God!" the couple exclaimed. "We were told that was Harry Truman in his 33rd-degree Masonic outfit."

"If you're not allowed to laugh in heaven, I don't want to go there."

—Martin Luther

"I'm convinced there is only one place where there is no laughter...and that's hell. I have made arrangements to miss hell. Praise God! I won't ever have to be anywhere that there ain't no laughter."

—Jerry Clower
from *Life Everlaughter*

A psychologist, an engineer, and a theologian were on a hunting trip in Canada. Seeking shelter, they knocked on the door of a small, isolated cabin. No one was home, but the front door was unlocked, and they entered.

They saw something strange. A large, pot-bellied, cast-iron stove was suspended in midair by wires attached to the ceiling beams. Why would a stove be elevated from the floor?

The psychologist concluded: "It is obvious that this lonely trapper, isolated from humanity, has elevated his stove so that he can curl up under it and vicariously experience a return to his mother's womb."

The engineer theorized: "The man is practicing laws of thermodynamics. By elevating his stove, he has discovered a way to distribute heat more evenly throughout the cabin."

The theologian speculated: "I'm sure that hanging his stove from the ceiling has religious meaning. Fire lifted up has been a religious symbol for centuries."

While they were debating the matter, the trapper returned. They immediately asked him why he had hung his pot-bellied stove by wires from the ceiling.

"Had plenty of wire, not much stovepipe," the trapper said.

—*Tal Bonham's Journey through Humor*

ST. MARY'S CHURCH		SACRED HEART CHURCH
	404 IRON STREET	
	HURLEY, WISCONSIN 54534	
	(715) 561-2606	
	VINCENT J. LYNCH	
	PRIEST	
Saints Created	Pagans Converted	Wars Ended
Elephants Fed	Crusades Begun	Lions Tamed
Dragons Slain	Pilgrimages	Cathedrals Built
Lost Sheep Found	Arranged	Seas Parted

Calling card of
Fr. Vincent J. Lynch,
pastor of St. Mary's
Church, Hurley, WI

"Preach the Gospel at all times. If necessary, use words."
—St. Francis of Assisi

"Through humor, you can soften some of the worst blows that life delivers. And once you find laughter, no matter how painful your situation might be, you can survive it."
—Bill Cosby

An Episcopal diocesan bishop went to an unfamiliar church to celebrate the Eucharist. There was a microphone on the altar, and being uncertain whether it was switched on, he tapped it gently with no result. So leaning very close to it, he said in a loud whisper which echoed around the church: "There is something wrong with this microphone."

"Don't call anyone sinners until *after* the collection."

© 1994 Harley L. Schwadron

The well-trained and responsive congregation, very familiar with the latest in liturgical language, replied at once, "And also with you."
—*Bulletin of the Parish of Coley, Halifax*

"From somber, serious, sullen saints, save us, O Lord. Lord, hear our prayer."
—St. Teresa of Avila (1582 A.D.)

While on a business trip, a Seventh-Day Adventist salesman, who is a strict vegetarian, stopped off in a small town and telephoned his parents, who are not vegetarians. When his father answered the phone, the salesman said he would like to stop by for a visit. The father yelled to the mother: "The prodigal son is returning! Kill the fatted zucchini!"

> *King David and King Solomon*
> *led many merry lives,*
> *With many merry concubines,*
> *and many merry wives.*
> *When old age overtook them,*
> *without too many qualms,*
> *King Solomon wrote the Proverbs,*
> *King David wrote the Psalms.*
> —via Charles J. Milazzo
> St. Petersburg, FL

"It is only believers in the Fall of Man who can really appreciate how funny men are. Love laughter, which sounds loudly as heaven's gates swing open, and dies away as they shut."
—Malcolm Muggeridge

"Christianity is the most humorous point of view in the history of the world."
—Soren Kierkegaard

FMC member Dr. John Gilmore begins his book, *Too Young to Be Old*, with a "Biblical Roster of Old Roosters and Hens" who cheerfully lived long lives.

Gilmore, who is pastor of Madisonville Baptist Church in Cincinnati, OH, notes that "Genesis 5 has more old men bunched together than anywhere else in the world."

Adam lived 930 years; Seth, 912; Enosh, 905; Kenan, 910; Mahahalalel, 895; Jared, 962; Enoch, 365; Methuselah, 969; Lamech, 777; Noah, 950. "Their fertility," Gilmore adds, "was as amazing as their age."

Gilmore also devotes chapters to the heroic senior women of the Bible: Sarah, who laughed at the birth of Isaac; Naomi, a senior who trusted God in tough times; Anna, a senior who bravely faced grief; Elizabeth, the mother of John the Baptist.

Gilmore observes, "God often entrusted leadership to old-timers at key turning points in history." Abraham was old when he began a nation. Moses was old when he led the nation, and lived to be 120 years. Neither of them ever retired.

"We ask ourselves if God can do anything through us when we pass into old age. The answer from God is that He can accomplish His purposes through those who we and others think are washed up and worn out."

Irving Berlin, who lived to the age of 101, was a Russian Jewish immigrant who wrote nearly 1,000 songs, including "God Bless America," "White Christmas," and "Easter Parade." Until the end, he never stopped making music. The aging composer once said: "The question is, 'Are you going to be a crabby old man or are you going to write another song?' "

NOAH'S MID-LIFE CRISIS

Tommy DiNardo of Florence, KY, is an engineer-turned-comedian-turned-engineer. The following reflections on Noah are from his audiocassette, *The Best of Tommy DiNardo*.

"I'd like to live as long as Noah lived. Noah lived for 950 years. He built an Ark, but it took him a hundred years. Apparently, it was a government contract.

"Nine-hundred-and-fifty years old. How does that work? Do you look like you're 100 years old for 850 years? Or do you look like you're 50 at 500?

"Do you go through a series of mid-life crises, or just the big one at 400? You know, wearing the gold chains and driving a sports chariot.

"Can you imagine Noah at 400 having a mid-life crisis discussion with his wife? 'You know, honey,' he says, 'I just want to do something different with my life. I want to make an impact.'

"His wife says, 'Well, honey, you talk to God.'

" 'Yeah, but so does Pat Robertson. I need something really different.'

" 'Well, you can always finish that boat you've been diddling with.'

" 'Get off my back!'

"What do you say to someone who is 950 years old? 'Noah, you look great! You don't look a day over 800, man! It's that fat-free diet, isn't it?'

"What do you say at the guy's funeral? *'Finally!'*?

"The Bible tells you everything, but it tells you nothing about what Noah did before he was a carpenter. I did a little research, and I found out that before Noah was a carpenter, he sold Amway.

"Noah was a heck of an engineer — that's for sure — building that huge boat. I was an engineer before I went into comedy. I switched when NASA built the Hubble telescope. Two billion dollars for fuzzy pictures of Pluto! Yeah, that engineer was a comedian, too."

"Forty days and forty nights of rain? What about the environment?"

© 1995 Goddard Sherman

From time to time, a well-known comedian confesses his belief that laughter has kept him living to a ripe old age. For instance, George Burns, Red Skelton, Bob Hope, Henny Youngman, Milton Berle, Danny Thomas.

Danny Thomas said, "Anytime I'm feeling old and down, I use laughter like a prescription. I laugh at life's problems and keep going."

The large number of FMC members who are in their 70's and 80's also suggests that there may well be a connection between humor and longevity.

"I live by this credo: Have a little laugh at life and look around you for happiness instead of sadness. Laughter has always brought me out of unhappy situations. Even in your darkest moment, you usually can find something to laugh about if you try hard enough. If I can make people laugh, then I have served my purpose for God."
—Red Skelton

"I could not be interested in any man's religion if his knowledge of God did not bring him more joy, did not brighten his life, did not make him want to carry this joy into every dark corner of the world. I have no understanding of a long-faced Christian. If God is anything, He must be Joy!"
—Comedian Joe E. Brown

"Fear can paralyze and even kill people. Fear, like misery, loves company. Faith and laughter are Fear's most formidable foes. Laughter cuts Fear down to size. Fear takes itself so seriously, but it shrinks when we laugh in its face. Poke fun at Fear and it goes into a frenzy. Why not resolve in this New Year to laugh at Fear?"
—Humorist Peggy Goldtrap
Madison, TN

"A merry heart doeth good like a medicine; but a broken spirit drieth the bones."
—Proverbs 17:22

A PRAYER FOR JOY AND HOLY HUMOR

A member of the Fellowship of Merry Christians, Roseann Alexander-Isham of Eugene, OR, wrote to the editor of *JN*: "I suffer from occasional bouts of depression. But each day I decide to be happy, and look for the small joys, and do something good for someone else if possible. I put a smile on my face and 'act as if until it becomes.' And it works most of the time. One day when I was in the pits, I asked myself, what should I pray for? I composed a prayer and would like to share it with you.

"Lord, grant me a joyful heart and a holy sense of humor. Please give me the gift of faith to be renewed and shared with others each day. Teach me to live this moment only, looking neither to the past with regret, not to the future with apprehension. Let love be my aim and my life a prayer."

~ *Chapter 2* ~
February

Tickling churches to life

B.C. **Johnny Hart**

An angel of the Lord telephoned the editors of four major national newspapers with this message: "God says the world will end tomorrow."

The New York Times carried a front-page headline which read: "**THE WORLD WILL END TOMORROW, RELIABLE SOURCE SAYS.**" A box read: "Analysis on page 11."

The Wall Street Journal's front-page headline read: "**WORLD ENDS TOMORROW; MARKET PLUNGES.**"

The headline in *USA Today* read: "**WE'RE GONE!**"

The headline in *The Washington Post* read: "**WORLD ENDS TOMORROW; CONGRESS APPROVES TERM-LIMITS, SCHOOL PRAYER.**"

A member of his congregation told Rev. Warren J. Keating, pastor of First Presbyterian Church, Yuma, AZ, that this was the best prayer he ever heard:

"Dear God, please help me be the person my dog thinks I am."

About 10 o'clock one cold February morning a man was in bed sound asleep. His mother came into the room.

"Son, it's time to get up. You gotta get ready for church," she implored.

"I'm too tired. Leave me alone," he said.

"Son, you gotta get up and get ready for church."

"I'm not going to church. Give me one good reason why I have to go to church," he protested.

"I'll give you two good reasons: one, it's Sunday and two, you're the pastor!"

—via Deacon William McAvoy
Lenexa, KS

On a very cold, snowy Sunday in February, only the pastor and one farmer arrived at the village church. The pastor said, "Well, I guess we won't have a service today."

The farmer replied: "Heck, if even only one cow shows up at feeding-time, I feed it."

The pastor obliged and did the entire service. As the farmer was leaving, the pastor shook his hand and said, "How did I do?"

"It was okay," the farmer replied. "But if only one cow shows up at feed-time, I don't drop the full load on it."

—via Ronald E. Leese
Spring Grove, PA

"Laughter is the sun that drives winter from the human face."

—Victor Hugo

"If we do not show love to one another, the world has a right to question whether Christianity is true."

—Francis A. Schaeffer

"It's a gushy Valentine's card from that church that wants to merge, saying, 'Can't the two of us become one?' "

© Cartoons by Johns

A group of women were talking together. One woman said, "Our congregation is sometimes down to 30 or 40 on a Sunday."

Another said: "That's nothing. Sometimes our congregation is down to six or seven."

A maiden lady in her seventies added her bit, "Why, it's so bad in our church on Sundays that when the minister says 'dearly beloved,' it makes me blush."

—Rev. Clifford Waite
Oakwood, Ontario

A missionary heard about a native who had five wives. "You are violating a law of God," he said, "so you must go and tell four of those women they can no longer live here or consider you their husband."

The native thought a few moments, then said, "Me wait here. You tell 'em."

—Tal Bonham, *The Treasury of
Clean Church Jokes*

*Adam's Valentine to Eve
Did not imply a choice;
The modern girls can pick and choose
From many charming boys.
His verse ran thus:
"Dear Miss, I'm Adam.
"I'm all there is to make you Madam."*

—Lois Grant Palches
Concord, MA

Gen. Larry D. Nelson, Chief of Staff, U.S. Air Force, said that one of the best jokes circulating among Russian political and military leaders a few years ago was that Adam and Eve were Russians. "They didn't have any clothes. They didn't have a house. They had to eat apples. And the Communist leaders told them this was Paradise."

"The trouble with many men is that they have got just enough religion to make them miserable. If there is not joy in religion, you have got a leak in your religion."
—Billy Sunday sermon (1914)

Helping his wife wash the dishes, a minister protested, "This isn't a man's job."

"Oh yes it is," his wife retorted, quoting 2 Kings 21:13: "I will wipe Jerusalem as a man wipeth a dish, wiping it, and turning it upside down."
—Tal Bonham, *The Treasury of Clean Church Jokes*

"How could Pastor Kermit ever forget the time Billy Graham's radio broadcast came through the PA system and he lip-synched the entire message."
© 1995 Steve Phelps

"Some visitors to Calcutta asked me to tell them something that would be useful for them to lead their lives in a more profitable way. I answered, 'Smile at each other. Smile at your wives, at your husbands, at your children, at all. Let mutual love for others grow each day in all of you.' "
—Mother Teresa
Heart of Joy

OUT OF THE MOUTHS OF BABES

"I was penciling one of my *Family Circus* cartoons and our little Jeffy said, 'Daddy, how do you know what to draw?'

"I said, 'God tells me.'

"Jeffy said, 'Then why do you keep erasing parts of it?' "

—Bil Keane

"Our small son Drew, who had been recently potty-trained, made this request during his bedtime prayers: 'God, please make my legs longer so I can get to the bathroom on time.' "

—Gayle A. Lasater
Yuma, CO

After the service, a little boy told the pastor: "When I grow up, I'm going to give you some money."

"Well, thank you," the pastor replied, "but why?"

"Because my daddy says you're one of the poorest preachers we've ever had."

An usher passing a collection plate in a church overheard a small child exclaim: "Daddy, don't pay for me! I'm only four!"

—via Catherine Hall
Pittsburgh, PA

"A friend of mine took her five-year-old girl to church every Sunday morning. Her mother always told her: 'We are visiting God's house.'

"One Sunday morning in the pew, the little girl asked in a loud voice: 'How come God's never home!' "

—Mrs. Harriet Husman
St. Petersburg, FL

A pastor asked a little boy if he said his prayers every night. "Yes sir," the boy replied.

"And do you always say them in the morning, too?" the pastor asked.

"No sir," the boy replied. "I ain't scared in the daytime."

—Tal D. Bonham, *The Treasury
of Clean Church Jokes*

The little daughter of a colonel living on an Army post was taken to church for the first time. The minister was one of the old-fashioned types who believed in illustrating his sermons with vigor. She stared in awe at the old minister, shut up in a box pulpit, thumbing the Bible and waving his arms wildly. Finally, unable to stand it any longer, she whispered to her father in a frightened voice: "What'll we do if he gets out?"

—Msgr. Arthur Tonne
Joke Priests Can Tell

"We haven't had any action from our letters to God!"

© 1991 Ed Sullivan

"Our pastor, Rev. Norman L. Dalton of Community Presbyterian Church of Deerfield Beach, FL, invited all the children to come down front on Sunday morning. His sermon was about 'The Holy' and he asked if any of the children knew what 'holy' meant.

"One child answered: 'Being holy means that you do what your mother ask the first time she ask.' "

—Randolph J. Shine
Deerfield Beach, FL

LINCOLN AS HOLY HUMORIST

From the wit and wisdom of Abraham Lincoln:

"Laughter is the joyous universal evergreen of life."

"Were it not for my little jokes, I could not bear the burdens of this office...With the fearful strain that is on me night and day, if I did not laugh I should die."

"I believe it is the inalienable right of a man to be happy or miserable, and I, for one, choose the former."

"They say I tell a great many stories. I reckon I do, but I have learned from long experience that *plain* people are more easily influenced through the medium of a broad and humorous illustration than in any other way."

"In regard to this great book, the Bible, I have but to say it is the best gift God has given. But for it we could not know right from wrong. All things most desirable for man's welfare, here and hereafter, are to be found portrayed in it."

"Men are not flattered by being shown that there has been a difference of purpose between the Almighty and them."

Col. Alexander K. McClure, a personal friend of Lincoln, said that "Lincoln's laugh was striking." McClure later published a book of *Abe Lincoln's Yarns and Stories*. Here is one of Lincoln's favorite stories:

A minister and a lawyer were riding on a train together.

"Sir," the minister asked the lawyer, "do you ever make mistakes while in court?"

"Very rarely," the lawyer said, proudly, "but on occasion, I must admit that I do."

"And what do you do when you make a mistake?" the minister asked.

"If they are large mistakes, I mend them," the lawyer said. "If they are small mistakes, I let them go. Tell me, Reverend, don't you ever make mistakes while preaching?"

"Of course," said the minister. "And I dispose of them in the same way that you do. Not long ago, I meant to tell the congregation that the devil was the father of liars, but I made a mistake and said the father of *lawyers*. The mistake was so small that I let it go."

In his book, *The Saints Among Us*, George H. Gallup Jr., reports on the results of a survey of 1,052 Americans whose aim was to identify living saints through a questionnaire of 12 questions. Ninety-three percent of the people Gallup identified as saints characterized themselves as "very happy." The "typical saint," Gallup reported, is an older black woman who lives in the South and earns less than $25,000 a year.

GEORGE WASHINGTON LAUGHED HERE
Entry in George Washington's diary:
"There being no Episcopal minister present in the place, I went to hear morning service performed in the Dutch Reformed Church — which, being in a language not a word of which I understood, I was in no danger of becoming a proselyte to its religion by the eloquence of the preacher."
—George Washington

After George Washington had his teeth pulled and his mouth fitted with wooden dentures, he had difficulty smiling — until he was refitted with dentures made from a rhinoceros' horn.

"Of all the habits that lead to political prosperity, religion and morality are indispensable supports. In vain would men claim the tributes of patriotism who would work to destroy these great pillars of human happiness...It is impossible to govern rightly without God and the Bible."
—George Washington

"George Washington, as a boy, was ignorant of the commonest accomplishments of youth; he could not even lie."
—Mark Twain

Four bishops were on a plane. During the flight, the pilot announced the loss of one of the plane's engines. "No cause to worry," the pilot announced. "We have three good motors working."
An elderly woman asked a stewardess: "Are you sure there is no danger?"
The stewardess replied, "No danger, ma'am. Besides, we have four bishops on board."
The elderly woman replied: "I would rather have four motors and three bishops than three motors and four bishops."
—Archbishop John L. May
of St. Louis

Two sailors were adrift on a raft in the ocean. They had just about given up hope of rescue. One began to pray: "O Lord, I've led a worthless life and neglected my children and been unkind to my wife, but if you'll save me, I promise I..."

"Hold it!" the other shouted, "I think I see land!"

—Margaret Harris
Grand Rapids, MI

Moses had a press agent named Sam. When he and his people got to the Red Sea with the Pharaoh's armies in hot pursuit, he called for Sam and asked: "Where are the boats?"

"Oh, I'm sorry, Moses," Sam said. "I was so busy with the press releases, newspapers and bookings, I forgot to order the boats."

"You idiot!" Moses exclaimed. "What do you want me to do — raise my staff and ask God to part the Red Sea?"

"Hey, boss," Sam said, "If you can do that, I could get you two pages in the Old Testament."

—Steve Feldman
Jefferson City, MO

A man took a fancy to a church notorious for its exclusiveness. He told the minister he wished to join. The minister sought to evade the issue by suggesting that the man reflect more carefully on the matter, and pray for guidance.

The following day, the man told the minister: "I prayed, sir, and the Lord asked me what church I wanted to join. When I told Him it was yours, He laughed and said, 'You can't get in there. I've been trying to get in that church for 10 years myself, and I can't get in.' "

"Give me, Lord, a soul that knows nothing of boredom, groans and sighs. Never let me be overly concerned for this inconstant thing I call me. Lord, give me a sense of humor so that I may take some happiness from this life and share it with others."

—Thomas More

On his television show, *Christopher Close-up, JN* consulting editor Fr. John Catoir elicited a bunch of one-liners from his guest, 79-year-old Jewish comedian Milton Berle:

Berle observed that "Bishop Fulton Sheen's television show *Life Is Worth Living* was my competition" during the early years of television.

"Bishop Sheen had the best writers — Matthew, Mark, Luke..." said Berle.

THE FAMILY CIRCUS

"We learned the fourth commandment: 'Humor thy father and thy mother.'"

Reprinted with permission of Bil Keane (*Count Your Blessings*)

"Bishop Sheen also had the 10 best one-liners: the Ten Commandments."

"Henny Youngman told me that when I was born the doctor slapped my mother."

Of another celebrity, Berle cracked: "He's very religious. He worships himself."

"Before I went on the air, I used to say a prayer every time that nothing would go wrong," Berle said.

"The only people here are the quick and the dead."
—Billy Graham, commenting on New York City traffic

When Mrs. O'Flaherty went into the confessional, she noticed an unfamiliar face behind the shutter. "You're not our regular priest," she said. "What are you doing here?"

"I'm the furniture polisher, ma'am," the man said.

"Well, where is Father Dolan?" she asked.

"I couldn't tell you, but if he heard anything like the stories I've been listening to, he's gone for the police."

In a hurry to make an appointment, a businessman parked his car in a prohibited area, and left the following note under the windshield wiper: "I've circled the block for 15 minutes. If I don't park here, I'll lose my job. 'Forgive us our trespasses.' "

Returning later to his car, he found a parking ticket and this note under the windshield wiper: "I've been circling this block for 15 years. If I don't give you a ticket, I'll lose my job. 'Lead us not into temptation.' "

Toward the end of his life, when he was suffering from the accumulated effects of a lifetime of drinking, an ill W.C. Fields was discovered reading the Bible by one of his friends. The astonished friend asked: "What are you — an atheist — doing reading the Bible?"

"I'm looking for loopholes," Fields replied.

"I'll bet St. Francis would've made up a happy little song to winter."

© 1994 Ed Sullivan

BULLETIN BLOOPERS THAT GNASH THE TEETH

From a church bulletin in Sherrill, IA: "10:30 a.m. worship Communion and candle lighting in remembrance of those who have died during the last year at both worship services."

—via Sr. Mary Owen Haggerty
Sinsinawa, WI

From a Magnolia, NC, church bulletin: "If you choose to heave during the Postlude, please do so quietly so as not to interrupt those remaining for worship and meditation."

—via Rev. Paul J. Davis
Scottsdale, AZ

From the bulletin of a Phoenix Baptist church: "Children's choir will now be hell on Sunday nights."
—via Rev. Dennis Daniel
Fountain Hills, AZ

In the bulletin of St. Lawrence the Martyr Parish Community of Chester, NJ: "There will be blessing of expectant parents on Sunday after all Masses. All expectant parents please go to the front pews and wail for the priest."

© 1993 Jonny Hawkins

FMC member Rev. Donald R. Jafvert, pastor of the Chapel by the Sea, Ft. Myers Beach, FL, once attended a continuing education event at Trinity College in Dublin, Ireland, location of the famous library which is home to the Book of Kells and other very old church manuscripts.

While visiting the men's restroom, he noted this message written on the inside of a stall door:

"This is a new door. The previous door, due to its literary capacity having been reached, was designated ISBN 0-37-078945-A and taken away for binding. It will shortly be published in paperback."

There was this nice lady mailing the old family Bible to her brother in another part of the country.

"Is there anything breakable in here?" asked the postal clerk.
"Only the Ten Commandments," said the lady.
                              —*Rumors*

David E. Sumner, a former editor of the newspaper of the
Episcopal Diocese of Southern Ohio, shared the following ads
which he once placed — tongue-in-cheek — in that newspaper:

The first Trappist abbot of Gethsemane was engaged in
conversation by a worldly unbeliever. "I never go to church,
abbot," the man said. "There are too many hypocrites there."
"Oh, don't let that keep you away," smiled the abbot.
"There's always room for one more, you know."
                              —Rev. Bruno M. Hagspiel, SVD

When God was creating the animals, a group of angels
remarked that it looked like fun, so God let them form a
committee and create one animal. The committee created the
platypus – an animal with the bill of a duck, the fur of an
otter, the tail of a beaver, and the feet of a frog.
"Enough!" said God, and ever since then there have been
no committees in heaven.
                              —Msgr. Joseph P. Dooley
                              Martins Creek, PA

"It's always a constant consolation to me to realize that
although God created man and woman, there is no recorded
testimony that he created committees. For this alone we
worship Him."
                              —John V. Chervokas
                              How to Keep God Alive from 9 to 5

"The only thing necessary to begin moving into the joy of the Lord is to tell Jesus Christ that you would like to be His follower. Receive Jesus Christ as your Savior and Lord, and He will give you the joy."

—Corrie ten Boom
to inmates in a
Rwanda prison (1974)

"Humor is the prelude to faith and laughter is the beginning of prayer."

—Reinhold Niebuhr

"Rejoice in the Lord always; again I will say, Rejoice."
—Philippians 4:4

A PRAYER FOR HOLY JOY

"Come and help us, Lord Jesus. A vision of your face will brighten us; but to feel your Spirit touching us will make us vigorous. Oh! for the leaping and walking of the man born lame. May we today dance with holy joy, like David before the ark of God. May a holy exhilaration take possession of every part of us; may we be glad in the Lord; may our mouth be filled with laughter, and our tongue with singing, 'for the Lord hath done great things for us whereof we are glad.' "

—Rev. Charles H. Spurgeon
English Baptist pastor
(1834-1892) via Rev. Edward A.
Black, Jr., Elysburg, PA

~ *Chapter 3* ~
March

When you fast, do not put on a gloomy look as the hypocrites do.
—Matt. 6:16

"You've confessed your sins with a contrite heart, Walter. Have confidence in the mercy of God."

As a Catholic, I've tried to explain Purgatory to non-Catholics. Purgatory is a place between heaven and hell. It's like you're stuck between floors on an elevator, and this elevator is jammed full of people who have just been to Taco Bell for lunch. You're going to get to that top floor eventually, but it's not going to be a pleasant ride. They understand that."
—Tommy DiNardo,
Catholic comedian
The Best of Tommy DiNardo

"In Heaven, there are no meetings. In Purgatory, there are long meetings three times a week. Hell is just one unending meeting."
—via Fr. George Birge
St. Rose Parish
Newtown, CT

The late Jesuit missionary Johannes Hofinger was intrigued by the Chinese habit of giving nicknames to people. The superior of the Jesuit mission in China was a dour Austrian with a sour face.

"Do you know the nickname the Chinese Catholics gave the superior?" Hofinger would tell an audience "Walking Purgatory." And Hofinger would add: "Please, my dear friends, do not be walking purgatories when you evangelize."
—via Rev. Harry E. Winter, OMI
St. Ann's Church
Fayetteville, NC

An elderly priest, who had spent 50 years preaching in parish missions, dreamed one night that he died and knocked on the pearly gates.

"Who is there?" St. Peter asked.

"I am Fr. Clyde, preacher of missions for over 50 years."

"Ah, yes, Fr. Clyde," St. Peter said, "I'm sorry, but you can't come in yet. First you will have to spend three months in Purgatory."

"Three months in Purgatory!" the priest exclaimed. "I spent my life preaching missions all over Australia!"

"Please be calm, father," St. Peter said. "You won't have to work. We have a comfortable chair for you in a comfortable room. You won't have to do anything except listen to your own sermons day and night. We taped all the sermons you preached at those missions..."

The priest woke up in a sweat.

—via Fr. Jim Carroll, OMI
Blessed Eugene
de Mazenod Parish
Burpengary, Australia

Deacon Sims comes down the aisle,
I wish Deacon Sims would smile.
Deacon Sims looks slightly bored —
Not like one who loves the Lord.
—Lois Grant Palches

"We carry our religion as if it were a headache. There is neither joy nor power nor inspiration in it, none of the grandeur of the unsearchable riches of Christ about it, none of the passion of hilarious confidence in God."
—Oswald Chambers, via George
Mettam, Wheat Ridge, CO

THE FAMILY CIRCUS

"Do I hafta do my homework?"
Reprinted with permission of Bil Keane

If you are on the Gloomy Line,
   Get a transfer.
If you're inclined to fret and pine,
   Get a transfer.
Get off the track of doubt and gloom,
Get on the Sunshine Track —
   there's room —
   Get a transfer.

If you're on the Worry Train,
   Get a transfer.
You must not stay there and complain,
   Get a transfer.
The Cheerful Cars are passing
   through,
And there's a lot of room for you —
   Get a transfer.

If you're on the Grouchy Track,
   Get a transfer
Just take a Happy Special back,
   Get a transfer.
Jump on the train and pull the rope,
   That lands you at the station Hope —
   Get a transfer.
      —Albert J. Nimeth, OFM

On their way home from attending an Ash Wednesday service, little Johnny asked his mother, "Is it true, Mommy, that we are made of dust like the minister said tonight?"

"Yes, darling," his mother answered.

"And is it true that we go back to dust again when we die?"

"Yes, dear," his mother replied.

"Well, Mommy, when I said my prayers last night and looked under the bed, I saw someone who is either coming or going."
      —Dennis R. Fakes
      Points with Punch

In *Pointer View*, weekly newspaper of the United States Military Academy at West Point, NY, the following passage appeared in a Lenten column by Rev. Robert T. Drummond, OSA, of Most Holy Trinity Church:

"As the (Lenten) season begins, Christians are signed with ashes...This act of submission is followed by a period of fasting and penitential practices and the removal of the sign of joy during religious lethargies."

—via Barbara A. Watt
Darien, CT

Before preaching his First Sunday of Lent sermon at the Immanuel Church-on-the-Hill, Alexandria, VA, Rev. Willie Allen-Faiella called all the children to the front and engaged them in a dialogue. He asked if anyone could tell him what Lent is.

An eight-year-old boy raised his hand and said, "Yes, it's what we get out of our pockets."

"I'm sorry Louise, but Lent is still Lent."
© 1992 Ed Sullivan

LENTEN RULES

I will:

* ✶ Not shriek at the children more than once a day.
* ✶ Stop making a pig of myself.
* ✶ Refrain from critical remarks.
* ✶ Stop smoking. Stop drinking.
* ✶ Let that poor driver pull into the line of traffic in front of me.

✶ Be nice to that checker, cashier, clerk, attendant, relative, neighbor, pastor, wife, husband, mother-in-law (circle one, several, or all).

✶ Cook that dish which my spouse likes and I do not; eat that dish which my spouse cooks and which I do not like.

✶ Put down that trashy book and read something worthwhile.

✶ Find out what the inside of the church looks like on a weekday.

✶ Get out of the sack every single Sunday morning and go to church; modify my Saturday night routine so that I can get out of the sack on Sunday morning.

✶ Give our Lord a little credit for the good things happening to me; blame our Lord a little less for the bad things happening to me.

✶ Blame my husband less. Blame my wife less. Blame everyone less.

✶ Say "thank you" more often. Say "please" more often.

✶ Talk less. Say more.

✶ Smile some. Try smiling even when I do not feel like it.

✶ Ask our Lord Jesus Christ to help me to do all these things.

—The Anglican Digest

"I thought sure this would be the Lent when his long-dormant spiritual values would come to the fore."
© 1990 Ed Sullivan (from *A Gift of Laughter*)

"The observances of the church concerning feasts and fasts are tolerably well kept, since the rich keep the feasts and the poor keep the fasts."
—Tobias George Smollett

"I think it's important that we Catholics preserve our identity. Penance is important. With the shortage of priests, maybe we should have a drive-through at our churches to speed things up for confession.

"You pull up in the family van. You got the whole family with you. The priest says over the microphone: 'In the name of the Father and the Son and the Holy Spirit.'

"You say into the microphone: 'Bless me, father, for I have sinned. I had a Number 5. The wife had a Number 9. My daughter had a Number 8. And my son had a combo – 5, 8 and 9.' "

—Tommy DiNardo
from *The Best of Tommy DiNardo*

For many Christians, Lent is a time for fasting and penitential sorrow over sins. But an early church saint, John Climacus (649 A.D.) spoke of Lenten disciplines as a "joy-creating sorrow" leading to the joy of Easter.

"God," he wrote, "does not insist or desire that we should mourn in agony of heart; rather it is His wish that out of love for Him, we should rejoice with laughter in our soul."

FMC member Karyn Buxman, a registered nurse, is determined to brighten up Lent. She led five Wednesday night Lenten programs called "Fools for Christ's sake" (1 Cor. 4:10) at Trinity Episcopal Church in Hannibal, MO.

She combined the Gospel and humor to teach church members that Christians should have a joyful outlook, even during Lent.

Writing in *The Arkansas Churchman*, Betty Rowland suggests that many of us might be well advised to "Listen for Lent."

"How hard it is to listen, really listen," she writes. "It's a habit, a ministry, a way of life. But it needs cultivating. Listen to your children, to your spouse, to an elderly person, to your pastor's sermon, to music, to the sounds of nature. Listen for God."

Why not give up talking for Lent?

The solemn saints discourage
Many folk from being good,
While the gaiety of sinners
Makes more converts than it should.
　　　　—Lois Grant Palches
　　　　　Concord, MA

"Modern investigators of miraculous history have solemnly admitted that a characteristic of the great saints is their power of 'lentation.' They might go further; a characteristic of the great saints is their power of levity."
　　—G.K. Chesterton

© 1995 Dennis Daniel (*Brother Blooper*)

Frowning is hard work; it takes 43 muscles to frown but only 17 muscles to smile.

"Could you talk to my niece, Job? She's going crazy because she has freckles."

© 1993 Ed Sullivan (*A Gift of Laughter*)

O St. Peter, Open Wide!

Monday I must make a salad
 For circle number ten.
Tuesday, Bible study –
 It's our turn to serve again.
Wednesday night is Mariners –
 We're in charge of chili;
Children's choir on Thursday;
 "Please send cookies down with Willie."
Friday's U.P.W. –
 I'll take chocolate cake.
Saturday, check doughnut order
 For post-sermon coffee break.
Sunday eve is Fellowship –
 Pizza I must buy
And although you see me smiling
 There's more than meets the eye
Because when day is over,
 I drop on bended knee;
I lift my voice toward heaven
 And pray most fervently;
O St. Peter up above,
 Those golden gates make wide
So that paunchy Presbyterians
Can someday squeeze inside."
                —Dona Maddux Cooper
                Stillwater, OK

Death And Taxes

Epitaph on a pastor's monument:
Go tell the church that I'm dead,
But they need shed no tears;
For though I'm dead, I'm no more dead
Than they have been for years.
                —Tal D. Bonham
                The Treasury of
                Clean Church Jokes

INSCRIPTIONS FOUND ON TOMBSTONES

Here lies the dust
of Marvin Peeper
swept up at last
by the Great
   Housekeeper

She lived with her
   husband
50 years and died
in the confident hope
of a better life

Here lies my wife
in earthy mould
who when she lived
did naught but scold.
Good friends, go softly
in your walking
lest she should wake
and rise up talking.

Beneath this stone
lies Dr. John Bigelow,
an atheist all dressed up
with no place to go.

William Jones
Beloved husband of Elizabeth
   Jones
Rest in peace until I come

Inscription on a dentist's
   tombstone:
When on this tomb you
   gaze with gravity,
Cheer up! I'm filling my
   last cavity."

Epitaph on a waiter's
   gravestone:
"God finally got his
   attention."

Pastor Ervin G. Roorda of the Third Reformed Church of Holland, MI, passed on the following epitaph found on a 16th-century Scottish tombstone:

Here lies Martin Elginbrod
Have mercy on my soul, Lord God
As I would do, were I Lord God
And you were Martin Elginbrod.

FMC member Pastor Joseph LoMusio of Temple Baptist Church, Fullerton, CA, the author of *If I Should Die Before I Live,* reports that he recently heard of a mortuary director who signs all his correspondence: "Eventually Yours."

"Rev. Doug Adams, a United Church of Christ pastor in Berkeley, CA, is renowned for telling the favorite jokes of the dearly departed at his/her funeral service. 'In counseling the family (after a death), I always ask the family what were the favorite jokes of the person who died,' Adams says. 'A funeral should be a place you laugh. Those who understand the faith know that death is not the end.' "

—via Beth Ann Krier
The Los Angeles Times

A gambler died. The funeral was well attended by his professional friends. In the eulogy, the minister said: "Spike is not dead; he only sleeps."

From the rear of the chapel a man shouted: "I got a hundred that says he's dead."

—Archbishop John L. May
of St. Louis

An inexperienced preacher was conducting his first funeral. He solemnly pointed to the body in the coffin and declared: "What we have here is only a shell. The nut is already gone."

—George Goldtrap
Madison, TN

FMC member Loren Swartzendruber, associate executive secretary of the Mennonite Board of Education in Elkhart, IN, tells this story:

"A fellow Mennonite pastor and I were in the last car in a funeral procession driving to a cemetery where I had never been before. We had been asked to conduct the service.

"It was pouring rain, and suddenly my car blew a tire. We couldn't stop the processional, which went on ahead, and we couldn't change the tire because my jack didn't work. A farmer came out but couldn't help us.

"Finally, we turned around, drove to a gas station with a funeral flag on the car and a flat tire on the front. My fellow pastor, wearing a Mennonite clerical collar, jumped out at the station and hollered: 'We're two preachers on the way to a cemetery, and we've lost the body!'

"They changed the tire like we were at the Indianapolis 500 and sent us on our way without charging anything."

Donald L. Cooper, M.D., of Stillwater, OK, a *JN* consulting editor who served on the President's Council on Physical Fitness and Sports, passed on the following story about a preacher who was on his deathbed:

The preacher called in his wife and children and said: "I know I'm terminal and don't have long to live. You'd better call my doctor and my lawyer. When I die, I want my doctor on my right and my lawyer on my left."

"Tonight we honor a man who gives new meaning to the phrase 'taking a moral stand.' "

© 1995 Ed Sullivan

His wife called in the doctor and the lawyer, and when everyone was assembled around the deathbed, one of the children asked: "Dad, why do we have to have your doctor and lawyer here?"

"Christ died between two thieves and I thought I'd do the same," the preacher said.

FMC member Jim Young of Gainesville, FL, produced this limerick, which he titled "It's Never Too Late to Make Up":

Alexander, the cheerful mortician,
with cosmetics is quite the magician.
For all sexes and races
he paints smiles on their faces,
so they grin as they go to perdition.

A melancholy man, always up on the latest accident and death statistics, once cornered Mark Twain. "Mr. Clemens," he said, "do you realize that every time I breathe an immortal soul passes into eternity?"

"Have you ever tried cloves?" Twain asked.

—Rev. Dennis R. Fakes

"A fine funeral was ordered for a woman who had hen-pecked her husband, driven her kids half nuts, scrapped with the neighbors at the slightest opportunity, and even made neurotics of the cat and dog with her explosive temper.

"As the casket was lowered into the grave, a violent thunderstorm broke, and the pastor's benediction was drowned out by a blinding flash of lightning, followed by terrific thunder.

"'Well, she's got there all right,'" commented one of the mourners.

—Dr. Francis Leo Golden

"Two preacher friends of mine were once called upon at the last minute by a funeral director to conduct a funeral as a team. Unknown to either was the fact that neither was familiar with the family. Arriving from out of town at the funeral home, they received instructions from the funeral director. Then the two preachers, side by side, led the coffin in a procession down the church aisle toward the pulpit area.

"Quietly, before reaching the front, one turned to the other and asked: 'Who is the deceased?'

"'I have no idea,' replied the other preacher. 'I was hoping you'd know.'"

—George Goldtrap
Madison, TN

Carl E. Wagner, Jr., of Baltimore, MD, spotted this bumper sticker on a car:

**LIVE SO THAT THE PREACHER
WON'T HAVE TO LIE AT YOUR FUNERAL.**

A newly appointed young clergyperson was contacted by a local funeral director to hold a graveside committal service at a small country cemetery in Iowa. There was to be no funeral, just the committal, because the deceased had no family or friends left in Iowa.

The young pastor started early to the cemetery, but soon lost his way. After making several wrong turns, he finally arrived a half-hour late. The hearse was nowhere in sight, and the workmen were relaxing under a nearby tree, eating their lunch.

The pastor went to the open grave and found that the vault lid was already in place. He took out his book and read the service. As he returned to his car, he overheard one of the workmen say: "Maybe we'd better tell him it's a septic tank."

—Rev. Leland C. Eyres
North Muscatine United
Methodist Parish
Muscatine, IA

The obituary editor of a Boston newspaper was not one who would admit his mistakes easily. One day, he got a phone call from an irate subscriber who complained that his name just appeared in the obituary column. "Really?" was the calm reply. "Where are you calling from?"

—Archbishop John L. May
of St. Louis

Comedian Milton Berle relates that he visited comedian Jim Backus, the voice of the Mr. Magoo cartoon character, in the hospital a few months before Backus died. Berle told Backus jokes for two hours. Berle recalled: "As I left I turned to him and said, 'I hope you get better,' and he said, 'You, too.' "

"When I reflect upon the number of disagreeable people who I know have gone to a better world, I am moved to lead a different life."

—Mark Twain

Seminary: A place where they bury the dead.

"Life does not cease to be funny when people die anymore than it ceases to be serious when people laugh."
—George Bernard Shaw

Not even approaching death could erase Winston Churchill's keen sense of humor. Churchill planned his own funeral and filled it with the promise of Easter. After the benediction, he directed that a bugle high up in the dome of St. Paul's Cathedral would play "Taps." Churchill then directed that immediately after the playing of "Taps," a second bugler, also in the dome, would play "Reveille," a call to get up in the morning.

I. R. S.

COUNT YOUR BLESSINGS-- AND THEN BE SURE TO REPORT ALL OF THEM!

© 1994 Harley L. Schwadron

"Faith can turn trials into triumphs and gloom into gladness."
—Winston Churchill

Bob Heltman of Hendersonville, NC, spotted this bumper sticker on a car:
"If God can make it on 10%, why not the government?"

"It's been suggested that the IRS post signs in its offices that read: 'In God we trust. Everyone else is subject to an audit.'"
—Charles J. Milazzo
St. Petersburg, FL

March 17:   St. Patrick's Day: the wearin' o' the green.
April 15:   Income Tax Day: the sharin' o' the green.

Lloyd V. Rogers, of Presidio of Monterey, CA, passed on the following story:

Then Jesus took his disciples up the mountain, and gathering them about him, he taught them, saying:

"Blessed are the poor.

"Blessed are the hungry.

"Blessed are those who mourn.

"Blessed are the oppressed..."

"I'm sure I can serve you better in this audit, Mr. Ames, if you stop humming 'A Mighty Fortress Is Our God.' "

© 1990 Ed Sullivan (*A Gift of Laughter*)

Then Simon Peter said, "Do we have to write this down?"

And Andrew said, "Are we supposed to know this?"

And James said, "I don't have papyrus with me."

And Philip said, "Will we have a test on this?"

And Bartholomew said, "Do we have to turn this in?"

And John said, "The other disciples didn't have to learn this."

And Matthew said, "Can I be excused?"

And Judas said, "What does this have to do with the real world?"

Then one of the Pharisees who was present asked to see Jesus' lesson plan and inquired: "Where is your anticipatory set? Where are your objectives in the cognitive domain?"

And Jesus wept.

Rev. Dr. William H. Willimon, minister to Duke University, Methodist pastor, and author of *And the Laugh Shall Be First* (Abingdon Press), tells this story about a young Methodist circuit rider who was sent by his bishop in the early 1800's to try to start a church in a town infamous for its lawlessness, murders, and beatings:

"The young minister entered the town's only pulpit with fear and trembling. He looked out upon two-dozen hostile, mean-looking faces. He was shaking so much that he could barely hold his Bible, but he went ahead and managed to preach his sermon. When his sermon ended, there was utter silence.

"Then, one of the meanest of the mean-looking characters swaggered up to him and said, 'Son, you don't have to worry; we ain't going to hurt you. But we aim to shoot that no good rascal what sent you here to us.' "

"These things I have spoken to you that my joy may be in you, and your joy may be full."
—John 15:11

DIETER'S PRAYER

Lord grant me the strength
That I may not fall
Into the clutches of cholesterol.
The road to hell is paved with butter,
Cake is cursed, cream is awful
And Satan is hiding in every waffle.
Beelzebub is a chocolate drop,
Lucifer is a lollipop.
Teach me the evils of Hollandaise,
Of pasta and gobs of mayonnaise,
And crisp fried chicken from the South.
If you love me Lord, shut my mouth.
                    —via Rev. Tom Walsh
                    Scottsdale, AZ

~ *Chapter 4* ~
April

The Easter Laugh
and
Holy Humor Month

B.C. By Johnny Hart

© 1994 Creators Syndicate, Inc.
Reprinted by permission of Johnny Hart & Creators Syndicate, Inc.

Scripture verse posted on the door of the infant changing room in the nursery at Wekiva Assembly of God, Longwood, FL: "We shall not all sleep, but we shall all be changed."
—Paul Thigpen
Springfield, MO

Message on a sign outside a Protestant church:
BEAT THE EASTER RUSH.
COME TO CHURCH THIS SUNDAY.

"Humor and laughter are a resurrection: they allow us to rise again and again."
—Harold Wessel

Sign spotted in a Washington, DC, church parking lot: "No Parking. Violators will be baptized."

Rev. Jon Erickson, a Lutheran pastor in Remer, MN, reports he saw the following bumper sticker:
IN CASE OF RAPTURE, I CLAIM YOUR CAR.

Mary Rose Betten, Catholic lay leader/playwright, was directing a children's Easter performance and overseeing the casting so that each child felt comfortable with his or her role. One boy insisted he wanted to be the rock in front of the garden tomb.
"Wouldn't you like to have a speaking role?" she asked him. But he would have no other.
The presentation went smoothly. Once again, she asked the boy why he wanted to play the rock.
His smile beamed at her: "Oh, it felt so good to let Jesus out of the tomb."
—Jean W. Spencer
Camarillo, CA

Pastor's Blooper: "This being Easter Sunday, we will ask Mrs. Johnson to come forward and lay an egg on the altar."
—via Rev. Hallack Greider
Anchorage, AK

FMC members Jeanne and Owen Welles, editors of the newsletter of the Florence (OR) Presbyterian Church, wrote an article about Easter. "Do you know how the date for Easter was set?" they asked their readers. "Easter is the first Sunday after the first full moon after the vernal equinox. Obviously, that was the work of a committee."

"Christianity has died many times and risen again, for it has a God who knows the way out of the grave."
—G. K. Chesterton

"Our theology should enable us to see God as one in whom we can trust, even in the middle of the ultimate fear which is death. If we can laugh in the crisis of death, that's one way of saying that God is in charge."
—Quaker humorist Tom Mullen

LAZARUS LAUGHED

"Thank you for printing Ed Sullivan's cartoon on Lazarus in *JN*. I did exactly the same thing in my little rural congregation in Niota, IL, about 10 years ago.

"Two nurses wrapped me completely in large Ace bandages. At the start of the service, I came down the sanctuary center aisle. When an elder gave the call to "Loose him, and let him go," the nurses came forward and cut

"The Bible-study class will love it, Dr. Lindvall. Now, when I shout 'Lazarus come forth!' you burst through the door."
© 1995 Ed Sullivan

the wrappings away. Then I proceeded to preach on the congregation's level.

"I suspect there was not a child or adult there that Sunday who has forgotten that drama or that sermon."
—Dr. Glenn Catlin
Church of the Beatitudes
St. Petersburg, FL

A certain doctor in Buffalo wondered why his practice was decreasing. He consulted a physician friend who agreed to spend a few days in the office and observe his methods.

After an hour, his friend had the answer. "Wilbur, you'll have to stop humming *Nearer My God to Thee* when writing out a prescription."
—Dr. Francis Leo Golden

AN ANCIENT EASTER HYMN

Join, then, all of you,
Join in our Master's rejoicing.
Rich men and poor men,
Sing and dance together.
You that have fasted
And you that have not,
Make merry today.
Christ is risen:
The world below is in ruins.
Christ is risen:
The spirits of evil are fallen.
Christ is risen:
The angels of God are rejoicing.
—Hippolytus, martyred theo-
logian (235 A.D.) from *Earliest*
Christian Hymns by F. Forrester
Church and Terrence J. Mulry

Spring bursts today,
For Christ is risen,
And all the earth's at play.
—Christiana G. Rossetti
Easter Carol

"Easter means you can put truth in the grave, but it won't stay there."

—Clarence W. Hull

The U.S. Postal Service affixed this yellow adhesive label on an envelope returned to a mailer because it could not be delivered:

KING380
920282028 3989
RETURN TO SENDER
CHRIST THE KING
MOVED LEFT NO ADDRESS
UNABLE TO FORWARD
RETURN TO SENDER POST DUE = $.25
10/21/89

"I read statistics every once in awhile, and it shows how church attendance is sorta falling off on Sunday mornings. I believe I discovered a way to aid preachers in getting people to church. Publish their pictures in the papers every Monday, instead of just on the day after Easter. There is no reason why people should have to wait from one Easter to another."

—Will Rogers

Humorist George Goldtrap, a Church of Christ minister in Madison, TN, said he was counseling a woman who was having marital problems.

"Does your husband believe in life after death?" Goldtrap asked.

"Hah! He doesn't even believe in life after supper," the woman said.

"I thought the Resurrection occurred only once. That sermon has been resurrected at least three times!"

© 1993 Goddard Sherman

FMC member Rev. Warren Keating, pastor of First Presbyterian Church, Derby, KS, tells this story:

There once was a very rich man who "wanted to take it with him" when he died. He prayed and prayed until finally the Lord gave in, but on one condition — he could only bring one suitcase of his wealth.

The rich man then began to worry, "What kind of currency should I bring — the dollar, the pound, the yen, the mark?" He finally decided that the best thing to do was to turn it all into gold bullion.

The day came when God called him home. St. Peter greeted him, but told him he couldn't bring his suitcase in with him.

"I have an agreement with God that I can take it with me," the man explained.

"That's unusual," St. Peter said. "This has never happened before. Mind if I take a look?"

The man opened the suitcase to reveal the shining gold bullion.

"*Pavement!*" the amazed St. Peter exclaimed. "Why in the world would you bring *pavement*?"

"I have always believed that God never gives a cross to bear larger than we can carry. No matter what, He wants us to be happy, not sad. Birds sing after a storm. Why shouldn't we?"
        —Rose Kennedy

Rev. Robert A. Pollauf, SJ, of Sts. Peter and Paul Church, Detroit, passes on this account of how Daniel saved his life in the lions' den:

King Nebuchadnezzar of Babylon was astonished that the hungry lions had not eaten Daniel. He summoned Daniel and promised him that if he would reveal his secret, the king would give him his freedom.

"It was easy, your excellency," Daniel said. "I

went around and whispered in each lion's ear —
'After dinner, there will be speeches.' "

Question: "What is the difference between a liturgist and a
terrorist?"
Answer: "You can negotiate with a terrorist."
— Fr. Rawley Myers
Colorado Springs, CO

In his book, *Angels Can Fly Because They Take Themselves
Lightly*, FMC member Dr. Richard Bimler, president of
Wheat Ridge Ministries, a Lutheran foundation, recalls a
time when he was invited to be a luncheon speaker. During
the meal, the president of the organization came up to him
and asked: "Are you ready to speak, or should we let them
enjoy themselves for awhile?"

"My pastor friend at Judson Memorial Church in Peoria,
IL, was accompanying a representative of the fire
department through the church building on the annual
inspection. After thoroughly inspecting the building, the
firefighter asked: 'Do you have a sprinkler system?'
"The pastor replied: 'Friend, this is a Baptist church.' "
— Rev. Al Abbott
Joliet, IL

"On the most joyful day of the year for Christians the
world over, celebrating Easter means looking upward.
Upward at the empty cross, the empty tomb, the risen
Christ. Upward at the promise of eternal life, of new life,
of joy.
"Some people live their lives as Good Friday Christians.
During one Easter Sunday service, one little boy asked his
mother: 'Why are all these people singing to their shoelaces?'
He understood instinctively that joy comes when you look
up, sing with a smile, and feel the good news."
— Jean Spencer
Camarillo, CA

"The empty tomb proves the value of Christianity; the empty church denies it."
—Rev. Denny Brake
Pomeroy, IA

In his book, *More Anguished English*, Richard Lederer reports that after an especially uplifting sermon, a parishioner telephoned her Methodist minister on Monday morning and said: "Dr. Remington, I have to tell you that your sermon was so stirring that I went home and had a change of life."

A newly appointed bishop, received by Pope John XXIII in private audience, complained that the burden of his new office prevented him from sleeping. "Oh," said the pope, "the very same thing happened to me in the first few weeks of my pontificate. But then one day my guardian angel appeared to me in a daydream and whispered, 'Giovanni, don't take yourself so seriously. Try laughing at yourself.' And ever since then I've been able to sleep."
—Edward R. Walsh
Westbury, NY

Classified ads in Rev. David Francoeur's whimsical *Ecclesiastical Times*, published irregularly in Gainesville, FL:

TAKE OUR PASTOR, PLEASE!

Midwestern congregation in thriving suburban area desperately needs new, creative clerical leadership. We would like to trade pastors with a congregation which wants a kindly but do-nothing pastor. We will pay you first year's package plus bonus for swift departure. Reply ASAP to: TET BOX 332-F.

MIDDLE EAST DIOCESE

looking for candidates for Bishop. Must be athletic, agile, and have great endurance. Former track stars preferred. Salary and benefits negotiable. Package includes bunker and armored personnel carrier for Sunday visitations. Must be willing to relocate. Interested parties reply to: TET, Box 12-V.

Billboard outside St. Dominic Savio Catholic Church in
Affton, MO:

SAINT DOMINIC SAVIO
CATHOLIC CHURCH & SCHOOL

Masses 7–8:30 — 10–11:30 a.m.
& Sat. 5 p.m.

COME EARLY & GET A BACK SEAT

A bus driver went to a church for the first time and sat in
the first row. After his sermon, the pastor went to the man
and asked him why he sat in the front row alone.

"Well," the driver said, "I just sat up here to see what you
did to make everyone move to the back."

—Msgr. Arthur Tonne
Jokes Priests Can Tell

Rev. Sidney Laing of Dublin, Ireland, got tired of listening
to the same old excuses from people who don't attend
church. At the end of his tether, he wrote the following item,
titled "Ten Reasons Why I Never Wash," for his church
bulletin:

★ I was made to wash as a child.
★ People who wash are hypocrites. They reckon
   they are cleaner than other people.
★ There are so many different kinds of soap, I
   could never decide which one was right.
★ I used to wash, but it got boring so I stopped.
★ I still wash on special occasions, like Easter
   and Christmas.
★ None of my friends wash.
★ I'm still young. When I'm older and have
   got a bit dirtier I might start washing.
★ I really don't have time.
★ The bathroom is never warm enough.
★ People who make soap are only after
   your money.

"It is by all means to be believed because it is absurd."
—Tertullian (160-230 A.D.)
(Early church theologian
referring to the
resurrection of Jesus)

"It is not only earth, but heaven as well which has part in today's (Paschal) feast. The Angels exult, the Archangels rejoice, the Cherubim and the Seraphim join us in the celebration of today's feast...What room is there for sadness?"
—John Chrysostom (407 A.D.)
from an Easter sermon

*For each species old Noah
  established
space sufficient for them to inhabit
  but they ran out of room
  with the Ark nearly doomed
from the habit of rapid young
  rabbits.*
  —Jim Young
   Gainesville, FL

© 1991 Doc Goodwin (*Phillip's Flock*)

"The resurrection consists not in words, but in life and power. The heart should take inward delight in this and be joyful."
—Martin Luther

'EASTER EVERY HOUR'

"The Lord's intervening, resurrection power is given not only for life's impossible problems, but also for our immense opportunities. There's always a time when we get to the end of our strength and courage and have to surrender the future

of a plan, project, or program. Out of the grave of our
depleted efforts, the Lord gives fresh vision, insight, and
answers we had not conceived of before. Easter happens
again. For resurrection living there is resurrection power.
This is Easter every hour, not a temporary fix, but an
intravenous feeding of love and hope from Christ's heart to
ours. This is living! This is enjoying God!"

—Dr. Lloyd John Ogilvie
U.S. Senate Chaplain
Enjoying God

"If we are silent about the joy that comes from knowing
Jesus, the very stones will cry out! For we are an Easter
people and 'Alleluia' is our song. Rejoice because Jesus has
come into the world! Rejoice because Jesus has died upon
the cross! Rejoice because He rose again from the dead!
Rejoice because Jesus has come to set us free! Rejoice because
He is the master of our life!"

—Pope John Paul II

On Easter Sunday, worshippers entering the sanctuary at
McMasters United Methodist Church, Turtle Creek, PA, were
greeted by two giant, red capital letters — M-T — flanking
the reredos behind the altar. M-T stands, of course, for
"empty," and the good news of the vacant tomb.

Rev. Jeffrey D. Sterling planned to quiz the children about
the M-T during the children's message early in the service.
With 28 brightly dressed little ones gathered around him on
the chancel steps, the pastor asked: "What's different about
the church today, kids?"

After a pregnant pause, Sterling's own daughter, throwing
her hands into the air, replied: "It's full, dad!"

End of sermon.

When a new building had to be constructed on Vatican
grounds, the architect submitted the plans to Pope John
XXIII, who shortly afterward returned them with these three
Latin words written in the margin: *Non sumus angeli,*

meaning "We are not angels." The architect and his staff couldn't figure out what the Pope meant, until finally someone noticed that the plans did not include bathrooms.

—Msgr. Arthur Tonne
Jokes Priests Can Tell

"Christian men are but men. They may have a bad liver, or an attack of bile, or some trial, and then they get depressed if they have ever so much grace. But what then? Well, then you can get joy and peace through believing. I am the subject of depressions of spirit so fearful that I hope none of you ever gets to such extremes of wretchedness as I go to. But I always get back again by this: I know I trust Christ. I have no reliance but in Him. Because He lives, I shall live also, and I spring to my legs again and fight with my depressions of spirit and my downcast soul and get the victory through it. So may you do, and so you must, for there is no other way of escaping from it. In your most depressed seasons, you are to get joy and peace through believing."

—Charles Spurgeon
19th-century English Baptist
pastor

THE FAMILY CIRCUS

"If you want them to grow, you hafta
say a prayer to your gardening angel!"

Several women were visiting an elderly friend who was ill. After awhile, they rose to leave and told her: "We will keep you in our prayers."

"Just wash the dishes in the kitchen," the ailing woman said, "I can do my own praying."

OUTREACH

FMC member David E. Sumner of Muncie, IN, who writes syndicated features for Episcopalian diocesan newspapers, reports that when you call one Episcopal parish in a major eastern city, you get the following message:

"Good afternoon. Thank you for calling St. _____ Episcopal Church.

"If you know the extension you wish to reach, touchtone callers may enter it now.

"For operator assistance, press 0.

"For a directory of priests and church offices, press 411 now.

"For a directory of other offices, press 556 now.

"For a recorded schedule of church services, press 555 now or hold for operator assistance.

"To leave a message on voice mail, press 333 now and then the extension number.

"Please wait during the silence."

"Now, let us return to the Lord the portion due unto Him according to that which we reported on Form 1040, line 23."

© 1991 Dennis Daniel (*Brother Blooper*)

"I go to sleep
"By counting sheep.
"I preach — to sheep
"I put to sleep."
　　　　—Msgr. Arthur Tonne
　　　　Jokes Priests Can Tell

"I have met worldwide a fellowship of joyous persons whose outlook and character are shaped by the reality and power of Christ's resurrection.

"They are men and women who take joy in the redemption and the renewal Christ offers, a company of believers of every race and color on every continent and of every walk of life.

"All have this in common: whereas like Saul of Tarsus they were once unbelievers who considered Christians a strange lot even if they did not openly persecute them, now like C.S. Lewis they declare themselves 'surprised by joy' a matchless, incomparable joy."
　　　　—Carl F. H. Henry

"The Christian should be an alleluia from head to foot."
　　　　—Augustine (430 A.D.)

When a bit of sunshine hits ye,
After passing of a cloud,
When a fit of laughter gits ye,
An' yer spine is feelin' proud,
Don't fergit to up and fling it
At a soul that's feelin' blue,
For the minute that ye sling it,
It's a boomerang to you!
—John Wallace Crawford
　　American poet and frontier
　　scout (1847) via Pastor John J.
　　Walker

"Next on Donahue — a couple who say they're a reincarnation of Adam and Eve and want to apologize for causing so much trouble in the world."
© 1994 Ed Sullivan

"April hath put a spirit of youth in everything."
　　　　　　　—Shakespeare

"I want to die with the heart of a child beating in my old chest and, God willing, I want to be remembered as a tiny seed that has been planted in the dark, that has roots in eternity and has died singing of the Resurrection."
　　　　　　　—Sr. Paulette Anne Ducharme

"Fully to enjoy is to glorify; in commanding us to glorify Him, God is inviting us to enjoy Him."
　　　　　　　—C.S. Lewis

"Be of good cheer; I have overcome the world."
　　　　　　　—John 16:33

AN ANCIENT PRAYER FOR CHEERFULNESS (CIRCA 590 A.D.)
"O God, who has folded back
the mantle of the night to clothe us
in the golden glory of the day,
chase from our hearts all gloomy
thoughts, and make us glad with
the brightness of hope that we may
effectively aspire to unwon virtues
through Jesus Christ our Lord,
Amen."
　　　　　　　—via Miriam R. Bischoff
　　　　　　　Zelienople, PA

Celebrate Holy Humor Month

© 1990 Fellowship of Merry Christians, Inc.
The Risen Christ by the Sea
Jack Jewell, artist

Jesus loves a good party. He performed His first miracle at a wedding reception in Cana, turning water into wine. In the parable of the Prodigal Son, Jesus tells us that the overjoyed father threw a big party for his returning son. "We are going to have a feast, a celebration," the father declared, with tears of joy in his eyes, "because this son of mine was dead and has come to life; he was lost and is found." (Luke 15:23-24)

In 1988, observing that the celebration of Easter had been sorely neglected in Western Christianity, the Fellowship of Merry Christians began encouraging churches and prayer groups to celebrate April as Holy Humor Month – starting with April Fools' Day – and to resurrect the old Christian customs of Easter Monday and "Bright Sunday" (the Sunday after Easter Sunday) festivities.

In Catholic, Orthodox, and Protestant countries, Easter Monday traditionally was observed by the faithful as "a day of joy and laughter" with parties and picnics to celebrate Jesus' resurrection. It also has been called "Bright Monday," "White Monday," "Dyngus Day," and "Emmaus Day" in various countries.

The faithful played practical jokes on each other, drenched each other with water, sang, and danced. It was a time for clergy and lay people to tell jokes and to have fun.

The custom of Easter Monday and Bright Sunday celebrations may be rooted in the musings of early church theologians like Augustine, Gregory of Nyssa, and John Chrysostom that God played a practical joke on the devil by raising Jesus from the dead. FMC member Rev. Donald B. Strobe, former pastor of the First United Methodist Church in Ann Arbor, MI, describes Easter as "God's supreme joke played on that old impostor, death."

"*Risus paschalis* – the Easter laugh," the early theologians called it. And the theme has echoed down through the centuries. St. Francis of Assisi advised: "Leave sadness to the devil. The devil has reason to be sad." Meister Eckhart, a 13th-century Christian mystic, wrote: "God laughed and begat the Son. Together they laughed and begat the Holy Spirit. And from the laughter of the Three, the universe was born."

Martin Luther wrote: "God is not a God of sadness, but the devil is. Christ is a God of joy. It is pleasing to the dear God whenever thou rejoicest or laughest from the bottom of thy heart." John Wesley said: "Sour godliness is the devil's religion."

FMC has urged Christians to begin Holy Humor Month by following the Apostle Paul's admonition to be "fools for Christ's sake" (1 Cor. 4:10) on April Fools' Day. *JN* consulting editor Dr. Terry L. Lindvall, an authority on the wit and humor of C.S. Lewis, suggested that April Fools' Day should be put in the calendar of the Christian year.

Wrote Lindvall: "There are two kinds of fools in the world: damned fools and what Paul calls 'fools for Christ's sake.' Paul himself is the one who legitimizes April Fools' Day for Christians. The cross is foolishness to those who do not believe; it is salvation, hope, love, and joy to those who do. It is a divine joke on Satan, the great deceiver.

"April Fools' Day, in most years, is a day of preparation for the divine folly of the Easter surprise. April Fools' Day offers a choice to us. Presently, we are all fools. The choice lies in for whom we play the fool: for ourselves or for Christ."

Christianity, in fact, has a long history of "holy fools," and many of them, like the 16th-century Italian Philip Neri, who "treated solemnity as if it were a vice," were regarded as saints.

From the fourth century onward, the holy fool has been a recurring figure in Greek and Russian Christianity. Russian Christianity has a long history of "holy fools" who dared to needle the Czars and the Communist bureaucrats, and who were esteemed by the people as healers and peacemakers.

In American Christianity, the holy fool has appeared in growing numbers in the guise of Christian clowns with clown ministries to hospitals, nursing homes, orphanages, and prisons. Many of these clowns are members of FMC.

G.K. Chesterton wrote: "Carlyle said that men were mostly fools. Christianity, with a surer and more reverent realism, says that they are all fools. This doctrine is sometimes called the doctrine of original sin. It may also be described as the doctrine of equality of men."

Responding to FMC's invitation, the First Presbyterian Church of Casa Grande, AZ, decided to celebrate "All Fools' Day" when a Sunday fell on April 2. FMC member Rev. Rick Lemberg's sermon was titled "Fools for Christ" and the Scripture reading was based on 1 Cor. 1:18-25. The service was designed with several practical jokes.

"The Resurrection is always an extra-special event for Chuck."
© 1994 Ed Sullivan

"We started with a practical joke on the song leader," Lemberg reported. "Without her knowledge, the congregation had been asked not to sing the first verse of a hymn. She began leading the hymn and wound up singing a solo until she realized what was happening."

When Rev. Lemberg went up to preach and opened his sermon folder, he found a note announcing that the senior high youth group had kidnapped the sermon, and if he wanted it back, he'd have to sing "Jesus Loves Me" to the congregation.

On a Palm Sunday evening, St. David's Episcopal Church in Topeka, KS, revived a medieval festival and hosted a "Feast of Fools" that included a circus, clowns, games, songs, and a traditional circus supper.

Everyone was invited to put on a clown face. Make-up was provided.

FMC member Rev. Robert Layne, basing his sermon on Paul's exhortation that we be "Fools for Christ's sake," observed that on Palm Sunday "Jesus is declared king, entering Jerusalem with no signs of kingly pomp or power, but riding alone on a lowly donkey, a seeming comic pretender. He is greeted with 'Hosanna!' by the faithful...

"To sing and laugh in festival before the awesome threats of worldly power can never be tolerated. The world always solemnly attempts to silence those who laugh at its sinister self-centeredness."

APRIL FOOLS' DAY MEDITATIONS

"April 1 is the day upon which we are reminded of what we are on the other three-hundred and sixty-four."
—Mark Twain

"I am to be a new kind of fool in this world."
—St. Francis of Assisi

"Wise men learn more from fools than fools from wise men."
—Marcus Cato

"The greatest lesson in life is to know that even fools are right sometimes."
—Winston Churchill

"There are more fools than wise men, and even in the wise man himself there is more folly than wisdom."
—Nicholas Chamfort

"A fool who knows his foolishness is wise; but a fool who thinks himself wise, he is a fool indeed."
—Dhammapada

"It is better to remain silent and be thought a fool than to speak and remove all doubt."
—Socrates

"Even a fool who keeps silent is considered wise."
—Proverbs 17:28

"Now verse 33 is one of the most difficult and controversial passages in the whole Bible. So let's go on to verse 34."

© 1993 Dennis Daniel (*Brother Blooper*)

"The jawbone of an ass is just as dangerous a weapon today as it was in Samson's time."
—James R. Swanson
The Pastors Confidential

"Young men think old men are fools; but old men know young men are fools."
—George Chapman

"George Santayana said that the young person who has not wept is a savage, and the old person who will not laugh is a fool."
—Pastor Denny Brake
Raleigh, NC

"We must live together as brothers or perish together as fools."
—Rev. Martin Luther King, Jr.

"Advice is that which the wise don't need, and the fool won't take."
—via Rev. John J. Kelly
Tracy, CA

"I just asked it for a list of scriptural verses commonly quoted out of context."
© 1992 Wendell W. Simons

"Take all the fools out of this world, and there wouldn't be any fun or profit living in it. God save the fools, and don't let them run out, for if it weren't for them, wise men couldn't get a living."
—Josh Billings

The budget here is very sound.
Donations come from all around.

Offerings keep going up!
Like an overflowing cup.

"Giving extra" — that's the rule.
There's too much money —
April Fool!

An original poem by FMC member Pastor Ralph J. Mineo of St. Luke's Evangelical Lutheran Church, North Baltimore, OH.

"This isn't the Starship Enterprise and I'm not Scotty, but you were beamed up."
© 1994 M. Larry Zanco

'THE LAUGHTER OF THE REDEEMED'

At Eastertide, wrote Protestant theologian Jurgen Moltmann, began "the laughing of the redeemed, the dancing of the liberated. Even in the days of Protestant orthodoxy, Easter sermons used to begin with a joke."

An FMC member, Episcopal Bishop William C. Frey of Ambridge, PA, writes: "What, after all, is a joke? Isn't it something that turns the tables on the expected, something that hinges on the unpredictable or unreasonable? There's nothing more unreasonable than the resurrection of Jesus. And to believe in it is to be part of that huge practical joke that God plays on those who trust blindly in the sufficiency of human reason to unravel all problems and to answer every question."

In an April, 1994, sermon titled "And Jesus Laughed," FMC member Rev. Frank Yates of St. Luke Presbyterian Church, Amarillo, TX, noted that Paul's letter to the Corinthians tells of Jesus' resurrection appearance to 500-plus persons.

Yates asked: "How would 500-plus people react to an appearance by Jesus, the one who had been crucified and buried? Would they applaud politely? My guess is that 500-plus folks rose to their feet with a standing ovation. This was the most incredible comeback story of all time. They would have jumped for joy and hugged their neighbors. These 500-plus folks, because of Jesus, had the best belly laugh of their lives. Easter had taught the 500-plus how to celebrate.

"Easter is the morning when the Lord laughs out loud, laughs at all the things that snuff out joy, all the things that pretend to be all-powerful, like cruelty and madness and despair and evil, and most especially, that great pretender, death. Jesus sweeps them away with His wonderful resurrection laughter."

Church historians indicate that there is considerable evidence that during the early centuries of Christianity, Easter celebrations went on for days and even weeks. But in modern times, these celebrations have faded away. Clergy and lay people who have lost faith in the resurrection are scarcely motivated to lead churches in ongoing celebrations of the resurrection.

Occasionally, one will come across a Greek Orthodox or Slavic or Byzantine Catholic church that still observes the old-country customs. FMC member Rev. George Mihalke, pastor of Holy Trinity Byzantine Catholic Church, Sykesville, PA, wrote *JN*:

"In our parish we have managed to maintain the joy of our ancestors during the Easter celebration. On Bright Monday and Tuesday we chase each other around after the services, drenching and being drenched with water. It's quite a sight – the women pursuing their pastor (in his cassock) down the street and around the grounds, drenching him with water. I'm sure the neighbors think us quite mad! On the second Sunday of Easter, we have a big party with much food and dancing, Slavic style."

There has been a revival of interest in these old Easter customs in Catholic, Orthodox, and Protestant churches in recent years.

St. Joseph Church in Kalamazoo, MI, has had large turnouts for Easter Monday ice cream socials. A group of St. Louis-area Protestants sponsored a "Resurrection Celebration," with music, fun, games, and comedy. It was hosted by humorist Steve Feldman, an Assembly of God pastor.

Other churches observed "Bright Sunday" or "Holy Humor Sunday" festivities on the Sunday after Easter.

North Bay Community Church of Clearwater, FL, began "Holy Humor Sunday" with a pancake breakfast. Clowns greeted people at the door as they arrived. During the service, the pastor, FMC member Dr. Allan R. Stuart, invited members to come forward to tell their favorite joke or anecdote.

The ushers played a practical joke on Pastor Stuart by arriving at the altar with empty plates after the collection.

At Westminster Presbyterian in Portland, OR, the choir wore their names and "numbers" on the backs of their robes on Holy Humor Sunday. Clowns greeted people at the door, and the opening hymn was done with a kazoo chorus.

After FMC member Rev. Bud Frimoth preached a sermon titled "Holy Humor," choir members stood and held up numbers like "9.5," "6.2," and "4.5."

Then Frimoth smashed two hard-boiled eggs on his head (an old Hispanic Easter tradition, but the Hispanics use eggs filled with confetti), and proclaimed: "Christ is risen!" The congregation responded: "He is risen indeed!"

FMC member Rev. Stuart A. Schlegel of Santa Cruz, CA, introduced "Bright Sunday" festivities at St. Luke's Episcopal Church in Los Gatos, CA. "That is traditionally called 'Low Sunday' for us, which I believe refers to the usually low attendance following the big turnout for Easter. But at St. Luke's Church Bright Sunday soon became a very well attended day indeed," he said.

© 1995 Jonny Hawkins

"I would save jokes from *JN* all year for this event. It was lots of fun, and so well received. Soon some of my clergy colleagues were introducing 'Bright Sunday' in their churches, and sharing jokes that brighten our lives."

David Neff, executive editor of *Christianity Today*, wrote to *JN*: "I wish more congregations could sense the *hilaritas* of the Easter season, rather than simply the dress-up pleasantness of an annual Easter Sunday visit to church.

"My own congregation, St. Barnabas Episcopal Church in Glen Ellyn, IL, takes seriously the penitential season of Lent. But the Great Vigil of Easter is then the high point of the year when, near midnight, the priest proclaims, 'The Lord is risen indeed!' and the congregation shouts its alleluias and sings the Gloria anew, all the while ringing bells which they have brought in order to create a joyous din.

"After the Eucharist, we repair to the undercroft for a feast of Easterish foods — egg dishes, breads, and wine. The Easter season does perpetuate this joy, the clergy regularly reminding us that Easter extends all the way to Pentecost, and the musicians singing Easter music in the service. You can tell I'm in tune with you on this."

A JOYFUL, LAUGHING, TRIUMPHANT RISEN CHRIST

FMC member Jack Jewell's painting, "The Risen Christ by the Sea," which appears on the back -cover and on page 65 of this book, is enjoying a phenomenal and growing grass-roots popularity. Many see it as a representation of "the Easter laugh" which church theologians have discussed down through the centuries — God's last laugh on the devil when He raised Jesus from the dead.

Hundreds of churches of all denominations have ordered the full-color prints from FMC and inserted them in their Easter Sunday bulletins, and their members have loved the gift.

The painting is appearing in church social halls, conference and retreat centers, church camps, religious schools, and hospitals and clinics all over the country.

A Protestant pastor contributed 600 of the prints to a public high school in Kansas, and the prints mysteriously appeared in a baccalaureate program at the high school. The graduates loved it.

Aboard the U.S.S. Enterprise, Catholic Chaplain James M. T. Connolly, USNR, an FMC member known as "Chaplain Bubbles" because sometimes he blows bubbles to illustrate his sermons, reported that "the painting is a real hot item in these parts."

A psychiatric clinic in the St. Louis area hung a poster of the painting in its lobby. Dr. Walter O'Connell, a Bastrop, TX, psychologist, hung a poster of the painting in his home "where I can contemplate while exercising. Some day, medicine will discover the importance of imagery for health."

Fr. Donald M. Byrnes, pastor of San Pedro Pescador Church, a parish of fishing families in St. Bernard, LA, ordered 600 of the prints, laminated them to make them waterproof, and gave one to each of the fishermen at the start of the shrimp season, when he followed the old tradition of blessing the fishing boats.

The painting depicts a strong, joyful, laughing, triumphant Risen Christ surprising His disciples at the Sea of Tiberias. Might He be suggesting, playfully, that His friends, who did not appear to be the most competent of fishermen, cast their net on the right side of the ship? That's where the fish were.

Translated from the Aramaic, the language of Jesus, John 21:4-5 reads: "When morning came Jesus stood by the seaside; and the disciples did not know that it was Jesus. So Jesus said to them, 'Boys, have you got anything to eat?' "

Might He be inviting us all to share in His laughter — the Easter laugh?

Might He be sending us an Easter message: that joy can be found on both sides of the cross?

Christians of all denominations have described "The Risen Christ by the Sea" as "startling in its intensity of joy," "riveting," "inspired," "beautiful," "powerful," "contagious in its joy," "healing."

When *The Detroit News* reprinted "The Risen Christ by the Sea" and asked readers in a telephone poll, "Do you think Jesus should be portrayed smiling?," eight of ten readers responded positively.

THE FAMILY CIRCUS

"This may be Good Friday, but Sunday's gonna be even gooder."
Reprinted with permission of Bil Keane

After interviewing 300 children across America, Associated Press Religion Editor David Briggs wrote: "One striking insight into the theology of children comes in their portrayals of God. When Christian children were asked to draw pictures of God, God and Jesus were invariably smiling."

The children — rich and poor, Catholic, Protestant, and Jewish — spoke "of a personal God who helps them cope with their fear of death, parental strife, the bully at school, and the death of loved ones."

Briggs noted that while many psychologists have been dismissive of the faith of children as childish, "a new wave of research is developing a powerful body of evidence that faith is a critical part of children's everyday lives."

The "Risen Christ by the Sea," interestingly, appeals to mainliners, liberals, and conservatives in all denominations. There is a poverty of resurrection art, and the popularity of "The Risen Christ by the Sea" may stem from that fact. We have poured over many collections of religious art, and we have been astonished by the lack of representations of the most joyful event in Christian history: the resurrection of Jesus.

Much of the artwork of churches of all denominations has focused on the passion and crucifixion of Jesus. Artists have tended to shy away from representations of the resurrection, and those few who have attempted it have captured none of its dazzling beauty, glory, joy, and humor – the Easter laugh.

Many representations of Jesus, past and present, depict Jesus – the Messiah whose message was "Be of good cheer" – as a tormented depressive. The Gospels, however, tell us very clearly that Jesus, far from being a depressive, was a healer of depressives. Jesus' awesome presence, both in His earthly body and in His resurrected body, brought great joy to multitudes.

FMC member Dolores Curran of Littleton, CO, a Catholic syndicated columnist, was delighted by "The Risen Christ by the Sea." She wrote: "Why does a happy Jesus make some people unhappy?

"We had statues and religious pictures everywhere on the walls of my childhood home. My mother clipped and displayed pictures of the Holy Family, Sacred Heart, Nativity, Crucifixion, Resurrection, and the Blessed Virgin.

"The pictures my mother chose were a good mixture of religious themes, but we had an elderly relative who hung only gruesome prints of the crucifixion, the bloodier and gorier the better.

"No gentle, loving Jesus with children around Him in this home. I remember being frightened at going into her home, a fear my older brother exploited by leading me into yet another room with, 'Wait till you see *this* one!'

"I thought of this aunt the past summer when I took to Ireland a stack of postcard-size prints of Jack Jewell's 'The Risen Christ by the Sea,' which I got from FMC's catalog. This is a full-color painting of a strong, joyful Christ surprising His disciples at the Sea of Tiberias. His hand clasps the ropes of a fishing net and his expression boasts a broad, triumphant grin.

"I took the prints to our cousin, a physician who, among other duties, serves the fishing fleets that call at the port of Killybegs in Ireland. He comes from a fishing family and is frequently called out to ships to treat injuries and illnesses. He liked the paintings very much and was pleased to have small prints to give his Christian patients.

"However, and this brings me back to my aunt, I saved a few prints for some old women who grew up in fishing families, thinking they would like them. They didn't. Oh, they enjoyed Jesus as a fisherman but they didn't like him as a happy fisherman. A couple of them looked at it, thanked me, and said nothing, but one glared at it for a long time and then said reprovingly, 'He doesn't have much to be happy about.'

"Clearly, a happy Jesus made them unhappy. I don't know where this need for a suffering-only Jesus comes from — and they certainly have a right to their image of Jesus — but I thank God my parents gave us the resurrected Christ along with the crucified Christ. Somehow, they knew that children need images of hope, joy, and celebration along with sorrow and death."

MICHELANGELO NEEDLED SAD-SACK ARTISTS

Noting the renovation of Michelangelo's famous frescoes in the Vatican's Sistine Chapel, FMC member Gina Bridgeman of Scottsdale, AZ, uncovered and passed on the following indignant remarks by Michelangelo (1564) addressed to his fellow painters:

"Why do you keep filling gallery after gallery with endless pictures of the one ever-reiterated theme of Christ in weakness, of Christ upon the cross, Christ dying, Christ hanging dead? Why do you stop there as if the curtain closed upon that horror? Keep the curtain open, and with the cross in the foreground, let us see beyond it to the Easter dawn with its beams streaming upon the risen Christ, Christ alive, Christ ruling, Christ triumphant.

"For we should be ringing out over the world that Christ has won, that evil is toppling, that the end is sure, and that death is followed by victory. That is the tonic we need to keep us healthy, the trumpet blast to fire our blood and send us crowding in behind our Master, swinging happily upon our way, laughing and singing and recklessly unafraid, because the feel of victory is in the air, and our hearts thrill to it."

Gina commented: "I'm sure Michelangelo would have loved Jack Jewell's painting 'The Risen Christ by the Sea.' "

The Fellowship has collected and offered in its catalog several other contemporary paintings of Jesus smiling or laughing, the work of both Protestant and Catholic artists: "Jesus Laughing" by Willis Wheatley; "The Joyful Christ" by Francis Hook; "Smiling Christ" by John Steel; and "Smiling Jesus with Children" by John Steel. These paintings, too, have become popular.

It is intriguing that, as the third millenium approaches, some contemporary artists are balancing out the many representations of a solemn, sorrowful, or stern Jesus with paintings of a joyful Jesus.

"God has chosen the foolish things of the world to confound the wise."
—1 Cor. 1:27

CLOWN'S PRAYER

This is "The Clown's Prayer" of Smiles Unlimited, a clown ministry to hospitals, nursing homes and prisons, based in Indianapolis:

"Lord, as I stumble through this life, help me to create more laughter than tears, dispense more happiness than gloom, spread more cheer than despair. Never let me become so indifferent that I will fail to see the wonder in the eyes of a child or the twinkle in the eyes of the aged. Never let me forget that my total effort is to cheer people, make them happy and forget at least for a moment all the unpleasant things in their lives. And, Lord, in my final moment, may I hear You whisper: 'When you made My people smile, you made Me smile.' "

~ Chapter 5 ~
May

'God has given me cause to laugh,' said mother Sarah at 90

THE FAMILY CIRCUS

"I'm tellin' Mommy. You're goin'
over her head."

Reprinted with permission of Bil Keane

"An expectant woman is often called 'glowing and radiant.' It's really sweat," says humorist-encourager Liz Curtis Higgs, the queen of the one-liner.

Higgs, a *JN* consulting editor, is a mother of two, a speaker who is much in demand by churches, and author of *Does Dinner in a Bucket Count?* and *Only Angels Can Wing It*.

"You've heard couples say, 'Some day we'll laugh about this.' Why wait?" Liz tells her audience. "Laugh now and save your marriage."

"The ideal woman was described 2,500 years ago in Proverbs 31 — and she's been intimidating her sisters ever since," says Liz.

"In nearly 40 years of living, a few of which have included cooking, I've never used more than four potatoes in a five-pound sack. Every few months, I carry another red mesh bag to the garbage can, arms outstretched, trying not to accidentally touch the waving tentacles."

"Good news! I'm married to a man who will eat anything. My husband, Bill, says: 'Hey, this is delicious! Can we have it again?' 'No,' I reply, 'I don't know what it is.' "

"What single women hear: 'Why don't you get out more? You'll never meet someone sitting at home. God has a man for you.'

"What married women hear: 'So when are you going to start a family?'

"What mothers at home hear: 'What do you *do* all day?'

"What working mothers hear: 'But who cares for your children while you work?' "

"I think it must somewhere be written that the virtues of mothers shall be visited on their children, as well as the sins of their fathers."
—Charles Dickens

TOP 10 PICK-UP LINES AT A SINGLES' CHURCH
  10. "Hi, this pew taken?"
   9. "My prayers are answered."
   8. "What's a charismatic like you doing in a mainline place like this?"

7. "How about we go over to my place for a little devotional?"
6. "Hi, angel!"
5. "Don't worry, I'm attracted to you purely in a spiritual way."
4. "I'm Episcopalian. What's your sign?"
3. "I think you're sitting on my Bible."
2. "Read any good Bible passages lately?"
1. "So, worship here often?"
—via David Briggs
AP Religion Writer

"The quickest way for a mother to get her children's attention is to sit down and look comfortable."
—via Pastor Ralph J. Mineo
North Baltimore, OH

"Mama says: 'What do you mean *Parental Discretion Advised*? How about a little *Network* discretion?' "
—Pastor Denny J. Brake
Raleigh, NC

Did Jesus laugh?
I think He did,
'Cause He was once
a little kid;
And all of us
Were made with joy,
Both sugar-spice girl
And snake-snail boy!
—Mary Wright McHarris
Knoxville, TN

Question: Why did the Israelites wander 40 years in the desert?
Answer: Even then the men would not stop and ask for directions.

The minister, leading prayers, was being carried away by his own exuberance. He began: "O Thou, who rulest the raging of the sea and calms the fierceness of the winds..." He then seemed to lose himself for a moment, but soon carried on: "...bless our wives."
—*The Desert Wind*
Scottsdale, AZ

HAPPY MOTHER'S DAY

The following reflections on motherhood by Catholic comedian Tommy DiNardo are excerpted from his audiocassette *The Best of Tommy DiNardo*:

"I don't want to hear any more talk about getting royalties from all the stuff being written about angels." ©1995 Ed Sullivan

"My Mom and Dad are good people. They are Catholic and very staunch supporters of family planning. I believe it used to be called the 'rhythm method.' I understand the main ingredient to the rhythm method was abstinence, which to me explains why the longer you're married, the better it works.

"My Mom had six kids — one planned baby and five rhythm babies.

"I used to ask my Mom: 'Did you really want to have six kids?'

"She'd say: 'Man proposes; God disposes.'

" 'Come on, Mom,' I'd say. 'Did you really want six?'

" 'No matter how many children you have, it's always just the right amount,' she said. Of course, that was when she was in a good mood.

"When we were driving her crazy, she'd yell: 'Because God wanted to punish me, that's why!!'

"'I just thought I'd ask.' "

"I was watching this talk show the
other day, and there was this guest
who said she has a 'multiple
personality disorder.' She said she
had several different personalities
living in one body. She said she had
raised an entire family, and her kids
said it didn't bother them.

"Her kids said the only problem they
had was finding the right Mother's Day
card — you know, the one that says
'From all of us to all of you.' "

"WOWWW! Say a prayer
that we can stay up here
forever, Mom!"
© 1995 Ed Sullivan

THE GIFT

Sense of humor; God's great gift
Causes spirits to uplift,
Helps to make our bodies mend;
Lightens burdens; cheers a friend;
Tickles children; elders grin
At this warmth that glows within;
Surely in the Great Hereafter
Heaven must be full of laughter!
                    —Eleanor Davies
                    Meadville, PA

Comedian Steve Allen passed on this story about George
Burns and his mother, which Steve saw in the *Epistle* of the
New York Friar's Club:

When Burns, now 99, was seven years old, he sang with
three other Jewish kids from his neighborhood in "The
PeeWee Quartet."

A small Presbyterian church in the neighborhood
asked the quartet to represent the church in an amateur
talent contest at a picnic for all of the churches in New
York City.

The boys opened with "When Irish Eyes are Smiling,"
followed by "Mother Machree," and won first prize — a

purple velvet altar cloth for the church and an Ingersol watch for each of the kids.

"I was so excited I ran all the way home to tell my mother," Burns recalled. "She was on the roof hanging out the wash. I rushed up to her and said, 'Mama, I don't want to be a Jew anymore.' "

His mother looked at him and calmly said: "Do you mind my asking why?"

"Well," Burns replied, "I've been a Jew for seven years and never got anything. I was a Presbyterian for 15 minutes today and already I got a watch." He held out his wrist and showed it to her.

She looked at it and said: "First help me hang up the wash, then you can be a Presbyterian."

"God could not be everywhere, and therefore he created mothers."
—Jewish proverb

The word "laugh" appears for the first time in the Bible in Gen. 17:17 when God informs the 100-year-old Abraham that his 90-year-old wife Sarah will give birth to a son. Both Abraham and Sarah laughed heartily. God commanded Abraham to name his son "Isaac," which in Hebrew means "God's laugh." After she gave birth to Isaac, Sarah exclaimed: "God has given me cause to laugh; all those who hear of it will laugh with me." (Gen. 21:6)

From Zvi Kolitz's book *The Teacher*, taken from the Talmud:

Rabbi Beroka used to visit the marketplace, where the Prophet Elijah often appeared to him. It was believed, as you know, that Elijah appeared to some saintly men to offer them spiritual guidance. Once Rabbi Beroka asked the prophet, "Is there anyone here who has a share in the world to come?"

"No," the prophet replied.

While they were talking, two men passed them by. On seeing them, the prophet remarked, "These two men have a share in the world to come."

Rabbi Beroka then approached and asked them, "Can you tell me what is your occupation?"

"We are jesters," they replied. "When we see men depressed, we cheer them up."

FMC member Merrilyn Belgum, age 71, bills herself as "the funniest old lady in the world." A widowed mother of six grown-up children, Merrilyn began her full-time career as a "sit-down comedienne" at the age of 62.

She was a social worker for 41 years — 21 as a faculty member at the University of Minnesota School of Social Work — before she decided to quit her job to pursue her dream of becoming a comedienne.

A member of Grace University Lutheran Church in Minneapolis, she often appears before church groups in a long, sequined gown with a stole of feathers, something out of the 1920's.

"I went to get my license renewed the other day," she tells her audience. "They asked me where I was born. I said I was born in iniquity and raised in sin. I should've just said I was born in Duluth."

When her husband died after a long battle with bone cancer, humor helped her family survive that difficult time, she says. "You don't get too old to be funny," she says. "Humor helps name the demons in your life. Once you name them, you can begin to cope with what life has given you. When you laugh, you get a glimpse of God."

FMC member Ardith Talbot, managing editor of Friends United Press in Richmond, IN, has a large collection of bizarre hats, going back decades, which she uses to illustrate her humorous presentations to clubs and organizations. This Quaker lady's favorite hat is a round, deep pink felt hat, which conceals a roll of toilet paper on her head.

On Valentine's Day, she says, she decided to do something special for her husband, Dick. So she got out a miniskirt she owned when she was a teenager. "It was OK when I tried it on," she says, "but I didn't know what to do with my other leg."

"It's never too late to have a happy childhood," says FMC playshop leader Sr. Mary Christelle Macaluso, R.S.M., Ph.D., also known as "The Fun Nun." Sr. Mary Christelle headed the biology department at the College of St. Mary in Omaha, NE, for 16 years before giving it up in 1980 to become a full-time, stand-up comedienne.

"When we built this place, you called it a 'window to God's country.'"

© 1995 Ed Sullivan

She founded a new order called "The Order of Fun Nuns." Each year thousands hear the Fun Nun spread the message that humor, combined with faith, can aid the healing of mind and body and help people face serious illness.

Sr. Mary Christelle does a lot of outrageously funny things. She once had 60 Presbyterians touch their knees and toes together, stick their tongues out, and sway back and forth, all the while warbling "Singing in the Rain."

She initiated a group of religion educators into the Order of Fun Nuns by having them recite "Mary Had a Little Lamb" with their right index fingers on the nose of the person to their right, and their left index fingers on the nose of the person on the other side.

"I'm one very happy sister," she says. "I'm out to change people's image of nuns."

"How often, as we sing of joy, I glance around the church and can't find one smiling face," writes *JN* consulting editor and playshop leader Gina Bridgeman of Scottsdale, AZ. Gina is the mother of two and a regular contributor to the annual devotional book, *Daily Guideposts*.

"What can we do to make church a place to walk out of feeling good about?" she asks. "How can we who fill the pews make it a joyful place, especially for visitors who may be wondering whether they should come back? Through some very simple ways, we can turn the solemn into celebration, and the somber into the joyful:

* Don't just stand there. Smile!
* Use God's gift of laughter.
* Be an aggressive fool for Christ.
* Come to the forefront of your church and suggest a more joyful approach to the basics."

"My soul magnifies the Lord, and my spirit rejoices in God, my Savior. For He has smiled upon me, His little servant girl..."
—Luke 1:46-48

BASEBALL PSALM

The Lord is my Manager;
*   I shall not quit.*
He maketh me to run
*   in green outfields.*
He leadeth me along
*   the straight basepaths.*
He restoreth my place
*   in the heavenly lineup.*
He leadeth me in reading
*   life's signals*
*   for His game's sake.*
Even though I walk up to
*   a volley of devilish pitches,*
I will fear no strikeout,
*   for Thou art with me.*
Thou dost promise me a bonus
*   in the presence of my opponents.*
Thou anointest my sore spots
*   with balm; my locker runneth over.*
Surely my statistics will be forgiven
*   me all the days of my life,*

And I shall dwell in
the Eternal Hall of Fame.
—Barbara Loots
Kansas City, MO

"Don't encourage these spirits, Mr.
Garagiola. We're here to exorcise them."
© 1995 Ed Sullivan

"If God let you hit a home run the last time up, then who struck you out the time before that?"
—Former Detroit Tigers
Manager Sparky Anderson

When they were both with the New York Yankees, Waite Hoyt and Joe Dugan were walking to Fenway Park in Boston one day when Dugan stepped into a church and lit a candle. That afternoon he hit 3-for-4 and the next day 4-for-5. The following day Hoyt, a pitcher, went into the church with him and lit enough candles to start a forest fire. Later that day, Hoyt was knocked out in the third inning.

"How do you explain it?" Hoyt asked Dugan. "You light candles and get a bunch of hits. I do the same thing and get knocked out."

"Easy," Dugan said. "I saw you light all those candles in church, but right after you left, I saw two gamblers come in and blow them out."
—Joe Garagiola
It's Anybody's Ballgame

Noting that the New York Yankees were interested in three players who had been suspended for drug use, Bruce A. Johnson of Grayling, MI, wrote to a *Detroit Free Press* sports columnist suggesting that Yankee Stadium be renamed "The Halfway House that Ruth Built."

"Lord, we know this game is only a temporal speck against the vast canopy of thine eternal economy — nevertheless, help us to beat the stuffing out of these guys."

© 1989 Dennis Daniel (*Brother Blooper*)

FMC member Scott McIntosh, pastor of the First Baptist Church in Swartz Creek, MI, wrote recently in his church newsletter:

"I must admit that I really enjoy myself during a worship service not only because I come to be with my Lord and His people, but also because some really funny things happen. For example, I can no longer watch the ushers from the back as they come forward to take the offering. It must be part of the Usher Training Course for them to stop in a semi-circle around the altar, spread their legs 18 inches apart, fold their hands in front of their belt buckles, and shake each leg twice before prayer. I've seen this repeated in most every church service I've been involved in, and the parallel between this performance and that

"Your father's back in church again. I think it was all those times he cried out to God when you wrote home for money."

© 1992 Ed Sullivan (*A Gift of Laughter*)

found in a men's restroom at a major league ballpark are too much for me."

Joe Garagiola, the commencement speaker at St. Louis University, passed on this advice to the graduates from his old friend Yogi Berra: "When you come to a fork in the road, take it."

The senior class of 1993 at River Valley High School in Three Oaks, MI, found an ingenious way to circumvent the 1992 Supreme Court ban on prayers at public school graduation ceremonies. After all the diplomas had been passed out at the May 28th commencement, an unidentified graduate deliberately sneezed loudly. In unison, all 95 graduates exclaimed: "God bless you!"
—via Rev. G. Patrick White
First Congregational Church
Allegan, MI

A seminarian named Breeze
Weighed down by MA's and PhD's,
Collapsed from the strain.
Said his doctor: "It's plain
You are killing yourself by degrees."

HURRAH FOR PENTECOST!

"What changed Jesus' disciples after the crucifixion from a scattered, frightened band of fugitives into the most remarkable collection of human beings the world has ever seen? *Joy* imparted by the Holy Spirit was what changed the disciples and knit them together at Pentecost. *Joy* was what Peter preached at Pentecost. And joy was the atmosphere in the early church.

"This was not the traditional hushed solemnity that has characterized so much of the church over the centuries. It was euphoria, hilarity, unspeakable gladness."
—Sherwood Eliot Wirt
The Book of Joy

A traveling evangelist always put on a grand finale at his revival meetings. When he was to preach at a church, he would secretly hire a small boy to sit in the ceiling rafters with a dove in a cage. Toward the end of his sermon, the preacher would shout for the Holy Spirit to come down, and the boy in the rafters would dutifully release the dove.

"Don't worry, Mr. Briggs. The side effects from this new Pentecostal joy you found should wear off any time now."
© 1994 Jonny Hawkins

At one revival meeting, however, nothing happened when the preacher called for the Holy Spirit to descend. He again raised his arms and exclaimed: "Come down, Holy Spirit!" Still no sign of the dove. The preacher then heard the anxious voice of the small boy call down from the rafters: "Sir, a yellow cat just ate the Holy Spirit. Shall I throw down the yellow cat?"

"Guilty!"
© 1995 Ed Koehler

"For God the Holy Ghost is the Paraclete, but what is a Paraclete? The word is Greek. Often it is translated Comforter, but a Paraclete does more than comfort. A Paraclete is one who comforts, who cheers, who encourages, who persuades,.who exhorts, who stirs up, who urges forward. A Paraclete is one who calls us on to good.

"A Paraclete is something that cheers the spirit of man, with signals and with cries, all zealous that he should do something and full of assurance that if he will he can; calling him on, springing to meet him half way, crying to his ears as to his heart: 'This way to do God's will; this way to save your soul: Come on, come on!' "
—Gerard Manley Hopkins
English poet (1880)

"Some churches have so successfully cultivated a somber mood that their sanctuaries resemble funeral parlors more than a place of celebration. Worship has the feel of a memorial service. If the Gospel really is good news, when do we get to shout 'Whoopee'? We should come to worship with the enthusiasm of one invited to a party, not the reluctance of one going to the dentist."
—Conrad Hyers
And God Created Laughter

"Some day I would like to visit that black church in Kansas City where, we are told, they have this slogan in their bulletin: 'Wake up, sing up, preach up, pray up, stay up, pay up, but never give up or back up or shut up until the cause of Christ in the church and in this world is built up!' "
—Anonymous
via Dr. John J. Walker
Post, TX

Headline in *Centre View*, a northern Virginia suburban newspaper: **Holy Spirit Now Officially Lutheran**. The article below it was about the organization of a new church, Holy Spirit Lutheran Church in Centreville, VA.

A minister was having difficulty preparing a particular sermon. He said to himself, "Maybe the Holy Spirit will tell me what to say on Sunday morning."
When at last he stood silently before his congregation, he

turned to the Holy Spirit for guidance. A celestial voice said
to him, "Tell the people you are unprepared!"
                                —Ron Birk
                                San Marcos, TX

A PASTOR'S PRAYER
Lord, fill my mouth
With worthwhile stuff
And nudge me
When I've said enough.
                —via Rev. Jack E. Musick
                Narrows, VA

THE KINGDOM OF GOD IS A PARTY
At the Chicago Sunday Evening Club, Protestant
evangelist Tony Campolo gave a talk called "The Kingdom
of God Is a Party," which was later expanded and published
as a book by the same title. Here are excerpts from his talk:
      "In Chapter 14 of Deuteronomy, we read that
      every year all Jewish families came to Jerusalem
      and brought with them one-tenth of all the money
      they earned that past year. And it was blown on a
      party!
      "Everybody was invited — the lame, the blind,
      the halt, people who didn't have any means of
      income, the widows, the orphans. There was
      singing, dancing, and a lot of food. Who wouldn't
      want to go to church if church was a party?
      According to Deuteronomy, church was meant to
      be a party.
      "God is a God who loves parties. He is a God
      who loves celebration. To all of us who are down,
      beaten, tired, and sad, He says, 'Come with me.
      We're going to have a party.'
      "When Jesus came on the scene, it was the same
      way. They asked Jesus point-blank, 'Tell us, what is

the Kingdom of God really like?' Jesus' answer was, 'The Kingdom of God is like unto a wedding reception.' A party!

"In the midst of the agonies of life, God wants His people to party. The church is about a Jesus who can take funerals and turn them into parties."

"Christians should be people who create fun and joy wherever they are placed."

"Faith always has as a companion joy in the Holy Spirit."
—Martin Luther (1546)

"If you, O Servant of God, are upset, for any reason whatever, you should immediately rise up to prayer, and you should remain in the presence of the Most High Father for as long as it takes for Him to restore to you the joy of your salvation."
—Francis of Assisi
via St. Bonaventure, SFO
Jacksonville, FL

"We are going to have a feast, a celebration..."
—Luke 15:23-24

PRAYER FOR GOOD CHEER

"O Father, save me from the depression that comes from accepting every gloomy prediction and every bad news story as though they were the whole truth. May your grace help me not to be anxious about tomorrow, but to live with the trust that enables me to cope with today."
—Reginald Hollis
The Anglican Digest

~ Chapter 6 ~
June

Fathers of fun
and the marry month of June

THE FAMILY CIRCUS

"Anytime you're ready, Daddy,
I'll be sitting outside growing older."

Reprinted with permission of Bil Keane

96

"My friends Erma Bombeck and Art Buchwald have done far more for the health of humanity than Madame Curie or Dr. Christiaan Barnard," says cartoonist Bil Keane.

There are those who would maintain that Bil Keane — creator of "The Family Circus," America's No. 1 cartoon panel — has done far more for the sanity of humanity than legions of mental health "experts."

"The Family Circus" began in March, 1960, in 19 newspapers, and now is read by 100 million people daily in 1,300 newspapers. Nice people can and do finish first, and you won't find a nicer guy than Bil Keane. Bil Keane is a lover; he loves people.

"The Family Circus" bears the mark of the deep religious faith of Bil and his wife, Thel. "I focus regularly on subjects often side-stepped by cartoonists: God, religion, prayer, church, and heaven," says Keane. "A happy home is as sacred a place as any chapel or cathedral."

Bil and Thel, who live in Paradise Valley, AZ, have five children who, when they were younger, were the inspiration for many of the adventures of Jeffy, Dolly, Billy, and PJ.

"One of the best ways to deal with stress," Bil says, "is to cultivate a sense of humor. So lighten up, friends! Help keep us cartoonists in business. He who laughs lasts!"

Father: "And when he proposed, did you ask him to see me?"
Daughter: "He said he had seen you, but he still loved me."
—Archbishop John L. May
of St. Louis

A zealous, newly ordained minister was assigned to a small, rural parish. In his first sermon he condemned horse racing, and the sermon went over poorly. A deacon cautioned: "You should never preach against horse racing because this whole area is known for its fine horses. Many members of this congregation make their living off horses."

The next week the new pastor came down hard on the evils of smoking. Again his sermon fell flat. Many of his members grew tobacco.

On the third Sunday the preacher condemned whiskey drinking, only to discover that there was a big distillery less than five miles from the church.

The perplexed preacher called a board meeting and cried out: "What can I preach about?"

The answer came immediately from a woman in back: "Preach against them evil cannibals. There ain't one of them within two thousand miles of here."
—Dennis R. Fakes

A FATHER'S PRAYER

"Our Father who art in heaven,
I am a father on earth.
You have given me this gift and responsibility.
Grant me the wisdom to carry it out.
Let me be there for my children when they need me,
And get out of their way when they don't."
—Adolfo Quezada
via Catherine Hall
Pittsburgh, PA

After a pastor's wife took her overworked husband to the family physician, the physician took the wife aside and whispered: "I don't like the way your husband looks."

"I don't either," she replied, "but he's always been a good father to the children."
—George Goldtrap

"Why don't you try prayer, sweetheart?"
© 1991 Ed Sullivan (*A Gift of Laughter*)

George Goldtrap of Madison, TN, a father and a grandfather many times over and a long-time favorite speaker in Church of Christ circles, is one of the funniest Christian stand-up comedians on the circuit. He's responsible for the cassette *A Funny Thing Happened on the Way to Church*.

At an FMC playshop, leader Goldtrap challenged another jokester to a joke-telling contest. He told the other comedian to tell his best joke and he would top it without saying a word. After his competition told his best joke, Goldtrap, without a word, bowed and with a sweeping flourish, removed his toupee. Goldtrap won, hands (and toupee) down.

A married couple was celebrating their 50th anniversary in a church social hall. The wife was smiling, but the husband had tears in his eyes. The wife asked the husband why he was crying.

The husband replied: "Fifty years ago today, your daddy put a shotgun to my head, and said that if I didn't marry you, he'd put me in jail for the next 50 years. If I had listened to him, I'd be a free man tomorrow."

—George Goldtrap

A charter member of FMC, Msgr. Arthur J. Tonne of Marion, KS, began doing push-ups and writing joke books in his early eighties. Now 91, he has written eight volumes of *Jokes Priests Can Tell*, and is currently working on his ninth volume of jokes.

David Letterman brought him to New York to tell some of his jokes on his television show. "I just love to tell jokes," says Tonne. "I never preach without a story, and preferably, it's a joke. Humor heals the spirit and it heals the body. Humor is an instrument with a power all its own."

A priest was talking to a group of Sunday school children. "And now," he said, "is there any boy or girl who would like to ask me a question?"

There was silence. Then a shrill voice asked: "Please, father, why did the angels walk up and down Jacob's ladder when they had wings?"

"Ah, yes," said the priest. "Now would any child like to answer that question?"

—Msgr. Arthur Tonne
Jokes Priests Can Tell

A woman who fancied herself to be a member of high society was seated next to a pastor at a community charity affair and decided to put the pastor in his place.

"Our minister," she said, haughtily, "is an Eagle, an Elk, a Moose, and a Lion."

"Indeed," replied the pastor. "How much does it cost to see him?"

—Msgr. Arthur Tonne
Jokes Priests Can Tell

© 1991 Ed Sullivan

"Why is it that talking to God is called praying, but when it's the other way around it's called 'schizophrenic'?"

—via Charles J. Milazzo
St. Petersburg, FL

"The world's toughest job — parenting — God gave to amateurs."

—George Mettam
Wheat Ridge, CO

Every summer, FMC member Bryan Townsend of
Talladega, AL, a father who describes himself as "a
motivational humorist," goes north to the foreign mission
fields — Illinois, Indiana, or Ohio — and helps build a
church with a group of men called "Carpenters for Christ."

Hugh Wiggins, one of the friends who goes with him, has
"a southern drawl so pronounced it takes him three syllables
to say dawg," says Townsend. He tells this story about Hugh
Wiggins:

"Once a preacher in Ohio drove us out to a building site
and said, 'This is where we want our new church.' He
picked up four rocks, placed one at his feet, walked about 50
paces in a straight line, placed the second rock at his feet,
turned at a right angle, walked about 75 paces in a straight
line, placed the third rock, turned again at a right angle,
walked about 50 paces and placed the fourth rock. He
looked at Hugh and said, 'This is how big we want it.'

"Hugh reached down and picked up a rock, threw it up in
the air and asked, 'Is that about tall enough for y'all's
steeple?' "

A man and a woman, who were friends for many years,
died and went to heaven. They told St. Peter they wanted to
get married.

"Take your time and think about it," St. Peter said. "You
have an eternity to think about it here. Come back and talk
to me about it in 50 years."

Fifty years later, the couple returned and again told St.
Peter they wanted to get married.

"Take your time and think some more about it," St. Peter
said. "Come back and see me in another 50 years, and if we
don't have a preacher up here by then, I'll marry you
myself."

—Rev. Paul R. Coleman
Zelienople, PA

A certain church found itself burdened with a very tedious
and self-centered pastor for a couple of years. Then came the

day when he was called to another church. He announced his resignation by saying, "Brethren, the same Lord who sent me to you is now calling me away."

There was a moment's silence and suddenly the congregation rose as one and began to sing, "What a Friend We Have in Jesus."

—Tal Bonham
The Treasury of
Clean Church Jokes

When a young minister was still single, he preached a sermon he entitled "Rules for Raising Children." After he got married and had children of his own, he changed the title of the sermon to "Suggestions for Raising Children." When his children got to be teen-agers, he stopped preaching on that subject altogether.

—Rev. Bernard Brunsting
Funny Things Happen

"And lately he just talks to me in parables."

© 1991 Goddard Sherman

JN consulting editor Sherwood Eliot Wirt of Poway, CA, was the first editor of *Decision* magazine, which he founded with evangelist Billy Graham. At the age of 85, this father still climbs mountains, rafts down the Colorado River, and writes books on Christian joy.

At age 83, he wrote an extraordinary book called *The Book of Joy*, in which he focused on joyful men and women of God through the centuries, including Francis of Assisi, Brother Lawrence, Billy Bray, Pecos Higgins, Corrie ten Boom, Grady Wilson, and Billy Graham.

"The Bible," he writes, "is a book of joy. There are 542 references to joy in the Bible. The Gospel of salvation in Jesus Christ is a passport to joy.

"The secret of Jesus was — and is — His inner joy. Our Lord had a merry heart. The most significant fact about Jesus that comes through in the Gospel accounts is His happy, radiant, loving personality, so different in character from the solemn religious types He was constantly encountering in His ministry. No one can mourn or weep for long when Jesus is around.

"What a pity that Jesus was not presented to succeeding generations as He presented Himself to his own!"

Dr. Wirt also observed: "Jesus came bringing a message of joy to the world, and where has it gone? The church of the late 20th century is committing a grave error. Part of it is thinking that renewal will come with threats of doom and judgment as people head for the hills.

"Revival will come when the churches of the nineties begin laughing and singing and loving each other, and showing the world what it means to know Jesus Christ. It will come when Christians are filled with the joy of His salvation as they wait for His soon return."

FMC member Rev. Ronald H. Weinelt, former pastor of St. John's Lutheran Church, Rincon, GA, is the founder and president of the Association of Battered Clergy (ABC). Says Pastor Weinelt: "I once heard a pastor say to a bunch of somber and serious Christians: 'You people look like you have received a life sentence in prison instead of eternal life with Jesus Christ.' "

FMC member Rev. John Gilmore, pastor of Madisonville Baptist Church in Cincinnati and author of *Probing Heaven*, writes:

"Can't you just once give me the money without your 'Root of All Evil' sermon?"
© 1995 Goddard Sherman

"Of all the activities humans would like perpetuated in heaven, laughter is high on their list. In a 1988 *Newsweek* poll 74 percent of those sampled thought there would be humor in heaven. A minority of 26 percent was opposed to any laughter in heaven.

"If you look back on Jesus' life, you'll see that his critics were always deadly serious. And the demons Jesus encountered, challenged, and expelled were sad sacks and sourpusses.

"Heaven's humor is going to be better than earth's humor. The French theologian Francois Arnoux (c. 1600) suggested that in heaven 'laughter never ceases.' Humorists will be at home in heaven."

In the midst of the Persian Gulf war, Marine Chaplain James M.T. Connolly wrote to the FMC office from his battalion near the Kuwait—Saudi Arabia border: "Holy humor really hits the spot out here. No glum chaplains need apply. The Marines and sailors I work with show a great appreciation for levity along with their liturgy."

Connolly's comment went all over the world. Associated Press Religion Editor George Cornell led off with the chaplain's comment in an article on FMC published in many newspapers throughout the country.

Connolly is known as "Chaplain Bubbles" to his troops because he blows bubbles in all sizes and shapes during his sermons to illustrate Gospel points.

"I've even constructed an incense-burning smokemaker so that I can do some smoke bubbles in church," he said. "Holy smoke!" he calls it. "Bubbleletics — the fine art of bubble-powered homiletics."

"Bubbleletics" catches the attention of the tough Marines he serves, he says.

"All goes well here," he wrote. "It's fun to watch the bubbles dance across the desert. Keep us in your prayers. And keep smiling."

Connolly, a Catholic chaplain, is now serving aboard the U.S.S. Enterprise.

"Our three-year-old daughter, Martha, was asking questions while my husband Dean and I were busily loading the car for a trip to the cemetery on Memorial Day to care for the family plot. 'What's a cemetery?' 'What's a grave?' 'Why do we bury people?' etc.

"I carefully explained as gently as I could. She became quite solemn, however, as she studied the flats of flowers, buckets, shovels, and spades we had put in the trunk and asked, 'Are we going to dig those people up?' "

—Jane Knuth
Portage, MI

"If you want to keep happy and healthy, try being an 'inverse paranoid,' " says Dr. Rich Bimler, a Lutheran pastor and father. "An inverse paranoid is someone who thinks everyone is out to make him happy.

"Try it. It works. Just imagine everyone you meet is trying to bring happiness and joy to your life. And then try to do the same for them."

Dr. Bimler, a *JN* consulting editor and president of Wheat Ridge Ministries in Itasca, IL, writes in his book *Angels Can Fly Because They Take Themselves Lightly*:

"You and I are called by God to be happy. To be happy does not mean that everything has to go right, and that problems and frustrations disappear. A happy person in the Lord is one who knows from where strength and comfort come."

He advises Christians to "live joyfully in the forgiveness that is yours each day."

IGNITING A MAN AND A WOMAN

A little girl in a Baptist church asked her mother, "Why do they rope off the aisle at a wedding? So the bridegroom can't get away?"

—Tal Bonham
Treasury of Clean Church Jokes

A cake decorator in New Zealand was asked to inscribe 1 John 4:18 — "There is no fear in love, but perfect love casteth out fear" — on a wedding cake. The decorator misread the verse, and when the cake arrived at the wedding reception, it was discovered that John 4:18 was inscribed on the cake. "For thou hast had five husbands, and he whom thou now hast is not thy husband."

—via Harold W. Bretz
Indianapolis, IN

"...for richer, for poorer, in sickness and in health, the baseball, football and golfing seasons..."

© 1991 Goddard Sherman

After a wedding, a teacher in a Catholic school asked her teen-agers the definition of marriage. A girl answered, "It's a sacrament which ignites a man and a woman."

In Ireland, a young farmer named Mike wanted to get married, and he and his Maggie went to the priest to arrange for the wedding. The priest prepared them with all the instructions and then said: "Now, Mike, do you want the new rite or the old rite?"

"Aw, let's have the new rite," Mike said.

After dressing up in his best suit on the morning of the wedding, Mike remembered that he had to feed the cows, so he rolled up his pant-legs and went into the barn. Then he went to church, but forgot to roll down his pant-legs.

As he began the ceremony, the priest whispered to Mike: "Mike, pants down, pants down."

Mike looked at him and said: "Father, can't we have the old rite?"

—Archbishop John L. May
of St. Louis

At a wedding, a pastor asked the groom: "Do you take this woman to be your wedded wife, for better or worse, for richer or poorer, in sickness or in health..."

"Please, pastor," the bride interrupted, "You're going to talk him right out of it."

A little boy was at his first wedding. After the service, another child asked him, "How many men can a woman marry?"

"Sixteen," the little boy said.

"How do you know?" his friend asked.

"The preacher said it — four better, four worse, four richer, four poorer," the boy replied.

—Rev David Polek, C.S.S.R.
Liguori, MO

Seating guests at a wedding, an usher asked a middle-aged woman who had entered the church: "Are you a friend of the bride, ma'am?"

"Lord have mercy, *no*," she said. "I'm the mother of the groom."

Former Education Secretary William Bennett attended a modern wedding where the bride and groom pledged, in their wedding vows, to remain together "as long as love shall last." "I sent paper plates as my wedding gift," Bennett said.

—*The Detroit News*

FMC member Msgr. Charles Dollen of Poway, CA, reports that a bride's notes on her wedding liturgy were found in the sacristy of a Catholic church. "Between the first and second readings," she wrote, "there will be the *Response Oriole Solm*." (Responsorial Psalm)

From the *Wellington Weekly News* in England: "The bridegroom's mother wore a two-piece purple and jade suit with purple accessories. The bride's mother wore a hat."

—*The Anglican Digest*

"Marriage is made in heaven, but so is thunder and lightning."

—Anonymous

In his homily at the nuptial mass of James Hornecker and Andrea Bede at St. Joseph's Church in Kalamazoo, MI, Fr. Ronald Mohnickey commented: "People are getting married everywhere these days — in hot-air balloons, on rafts… My favorite is on a roller coaster, because that says something about the way marriage is. But I'm happy that this marriage is in church." Then, turning to the couple, he added: "You'll need both faith and fun in a marriage."

"If it's okay with you, I'm going to use the short form."

© 1995 Ed Sullivan

"Left motherless at an early age, Henry Ward Beecher slept in the same room with a black man, Charles Simms, who was his father's farm help. The great preacher later spoke often of Charles Simms' influence on his life. Each night, Beecher recalled, Simms would set a candle at the head of his bed and 'pray and sing and laugh.' When we see Beecher standing in his pulpit dramatizing the horror of auctioning off a slave, we can remember the joyful noise of Charles Simms as he prayed and sang and laughed."

—Rev. James B. Bailey
First Presbyterian Church
Monongahela, PA

The English Baptist preacher Charles H. Spurgeon (1834-1892) gave this reply to those who have argued that the Gospels never said Jesus laughed:

"To me a smile is no sin, and a laugh is no crime. I never knew what the hearty laugh and what the happy face meant till I knew Christ."

"Once again your cheeks will fill with laughter."
—Job 8:21

"Happy are you who weep now; you shall laugh.'"
—Luke 6:21

© 1993 Wendell W. Simons

IRISH BLESSING FOR WEDDINGS

May the road rise to meet you.
May the wind be always at your back.
May the sun shine warm upon your face,
The rains fall soft upon your fields.
May the light of friendship guide your paths together.
May the laughter of children grace the halls of your home.
May the joy of living for one another trip a smile from your lips,
A twinkle from your eye.
And when eternity beckons, at the end of a life heaped high with
*   love,*
May the good Lord embrace you with the arms that have nurtured
*   you*
the whole length of your joy-filled days.
May the gracious God hold you both in the palm of His hands.
and, today, may the Spirit of Love find a dwelling place in your
*   hearts.*

                              —via *Apple Seeds*

~ Chapter 7 ~
July

In the beginning was Joy
Golf came later

Reprinted with permission of Bil Keane

"In the beginning was Joy. And the Joy was with God, and the Joy flowed within God. He willed that all things might come into being, that His Joy might fill all things. So God loved the universe into existence.

"The love that holds all things together by its limitless power was the Fount of Joy, the mouth of a mighty river that flows singing in superabundance from the heart of God.

"But the Adversary was near. Devoid of heaven's music, he was devoid of heaven's Joy. He lured the creatures' gaze away from the Face of God so that the floodgates of Joy were closed.

"But in the fullness of time, the Fount of Joy became flesh, and dwelt among us, full of light and song. By Him the floodgates were opened, the furrows dug again, until the hills themselves burst into music and the trees of the field clapped their hands."

—Paul Thigpen
A Reason for Joy

"My wife and I were at the beach. I said, 'You know, I'm 56. I'm middle-aged!'

"She said: 'How many men do you know over 112?'

"It seems that just as soon as my pimples cleared up, my hair fell out. I wish I had hair. If I had the gift of healing, would I look like this?"

—Evangelist Tony Campolo

"We have not seen you in the temple since you started hitting rocks with a stick."

© 1985 Ed Sullivan

FMC members Terry and Lane Buckner of Fort Wayne, IN, went to hear a lecture on Jewish humor by Moshe Waldoks, co-editor of *The Big Book of Jewish Humor* (HarperCollins). Waldoks told this story:

"A Jewish grandmother takes her favorite grandson to the beach. She puts a little sun hat on him, and gives him a pail and shovel. Then she lies down and falls asleep.

"She wakes up and realizes the beach is deserted. She sees the kid has been dragged into the ocean. She is beside herself. 'Oy gevalt! Oh woe! Somebody save my child!' she wails. The kid goes down for the third time, and she looks up to heaven and says, 'Creator of the universe, please save my child and I promise I'll turn to the righteous path.'

"Sure enough, the boy is deposited on the shore. She runs up, puts her head on his chest and finds the boy is breathing. She looks around and she gets this scowl on her face. She points her finger to heaven. 'But he had a hat!' "

"I've noticed that people don't get dressed up for church anymore. In Virginia Beach, it's kind of like people pop in to church on the way to the oceanfront. You know, you got your little daughter with an inner tube around her waist, and your son is taking up the whole pew because he's waxing his surfboard. Alleluia, dude!"

—Tommy DiNardo

"Remember our agreement. The first one who prays loses the hole."
© 1994 Goddard Sherman

A life-long golfer, FMC member Jim Reed, a United Methodist layman, retired from golf to Cotter, AR, where he now paints watercolors because, he says, "they require fewer strokes." He also wrote a book called *The Funny Side of Golf*. It includes a lot of jokes and anecdotes about golf, clergy, and church. Here are some of them:

A preacher felt badly because he had been defeated soundly on the golf course by one of his parishioners, a man 30 years his senior. "Cheer up, Reverend," said his opponent, "You'll win in the end. You'll be burying me some day."

"Even then," said the inconsolable preacher, "it will be your hole."

A golfer, having a bad day, went into a tantrum on the last hole. He swore, broke his putter, and said, "I've got to give it up."

"Give up golf?" asked the caddie.

"No," he said, "give up the ministry."

You can always tell a golfer in church. He is the one who uses an interlocking grip when he puts his hands together to pray.

Sunday is a day to bow our heads. Most do it in church; others on the golf course.

A golfing preacher, who too often committed the golfing sin of looking up too soon, started a round by suggesting that his caddie pray for him. The bag-toter watched carefully as the minister addressed the ball. "Are you praying for me?" the minister asked.

"Yes, sir," was the reply, "I'm praying, but you gotta keep your head down."

Sunday golfer: a person more interested in a hole-in-one than the Holy One.

A funeral procession passed slowly down the road near the eighth tee of the golf course. A player stepped back from the ball he was about to drive, took off his cap and bowed his head. When the procession passed, he put his cap back on, stepped up and drove the ball down the middle of the fairway.

"Well," said his partner, "that funeral cortege sure didn't interfere with your concentration."

"It wasn't easy to keep my concentration," replied the golfer. "After all, we were happily married for 20 years."

NOW, ON VERSE 3, ONLY THOSE SING WHO HAVEN'T BEEN SPEAKING TO EACH OTHER FOR THE PAST TWO WEEKS.

© 1994 Ed Koehler

A golfer's game was delayed by a thunderstorm, so he wired his bride-to-be waiting at the church: "RAIN HELD UP GAME. WILL BE AN HOUR LATE. DON'T MARRY ANYONE TILL I GET THERE."

Fr. Muckerman: "When you were abroad did you visit the Holy Land?"
Mrs. Woroniecki: "We sure did. My husband wouldn't leave until he played St. Andrews."

The way some golfers play, they would be better off in church.

An enthusiastic golfer died and went to hell. Accustomed to playing in the withering heat of Arizona, he asked the devil if he had golf courses.
"Certainly," replied the devil. "We have courses with grass greens and watered fairways."
"That's great!" exclaimed the golfer. "Now where are the clubs and balls?"
"We don't have any," said the devil. "That's the hell of it."

They say it's no sin to play golf on Sunday, but the way some golfers play it's a crime.

Bob Hope said, "Whenever I play golf with Gerald Ford, I usually try to make it a foursome — the President, myself, a paramedic, and a faith healer."

When asked where was the safest place for spectators to stand during a celebrity golf tournament, Joe Garagiola said, "In the fairway."

Pity the man who told his boss he was going to church for a funeral but went instead to the golf course and shot his first hole-in-one.

Franklin P. Adams defined middle-age as when you are too young to take up golf and too old to rush up to the tennis net.

Playing golf is a lot like raising children. You keep thinking you'll do better next time.

"I never pray on a golf course. Actually, the Lord answers my prayers everywhere except on the course."
—Billy Graham

"I'd move heaven and earth to break 10," said the golf addict as he desperately banged away in a sand trap.
"Try heaven," advised his partner. "You've already moved enough earth."
—Tal Bonham
Treasury of Clean Church Jokes

A certain rabbi had a weakness for golf. But he had no time for it. Searching his busy schedule, he found one day in a year's time when he could play. Unfortunately, that day fell on the Sabbath.

The rabbi apologized to God and traveled some distance to a golf club so that no one who might know him would see him.

As he teed up the first ball, an angel looked down from heaven aghast: "A rabbi playing golf on the Sabbath!" He immediately told the Almighty about it.

On the third hole, God sent down a gust of wind that made the rabbi's ball sink into the cup — a hole in one!

The angel watching was puzzled. "You call that punishment?"

"Think about it," the Lord replied. "Who can he tell?"
—Rev. Dennis R. Fakes

'GOS-BALLS'

An ad in *Christianity Today* introduced "Gos-balls" — Christian golf balls carrying Bible verses. You get four verses on a one-dozen set for $29.99. The verses (from the King James Version) are:

"Because strait is the gate, and narrow is the way, which leadeth unto life, and few there be that find it." Matt. 7:14

"But God is the judge; he putteth down one, and setteth up another." Psalm 75:7

"He maketh me to lie down in green pastures." Psalm 23:2

"I will seek that which was lost, and bring again that which was driven away." Ezekiel 34:16

Golf report from FMC member Roger Deem of Jacksonville, IL:

"While playing golf one afternoon, I was overtaken by a pair of youngsters. One was a member of the Sunday School class I taught. The other turned out to be the son of another denomination's pastor. I invited them to join me for the rest of the round.

"We began to discuss the differences between our respective religions, especially the rites of baptism. His faith calls for sprinkling water on the head while mine 'holds them until they bubble.'

"Hello, I'm Polly. Unfortunately, Rev. Wolter has come down with laryngitis. Fortunately, I'm in his study when he practices his sermons."

© 1994 Ed Koehler

"As our round progressed, we received what I believe was a sign from God that there are different strokes for different folks. One person's way of worshipping the Lord might not be right for another. The sign was obvious and unmistakable: On the same hole, the boy hit his drive under a fairway sprinkler and I drove mine into the lake."

"In the desert, two very different birds thrive. The vultures see nothing but dead and stinking carcasses. The humming-birds seek the lovely blossoms of cacti.

"The vultures live on the dead past. The hummingbirds live on the fragrant present. Each bird finds what it is looking for. So do people."

—Anonymous

"I think it is impossible to live and not to grieve, but I am always suspicious of my own grief lest it be self-pity in sheep's clothing. Altogether it is better to pray than to grieve; and it is greater to be joyful than to grieve. But it takes more grace to be joyful than any but the greatest have."

—Flannery O'Connor

"A vacation is when you pack seven suitcases, three small children, a mother-in-law, two dogs and say, 'It's good to get away from it all.' "

—Rev. James A. Simpson

Question: Who played tennis in the Bible?
Answer: Daniel — he served in Nebuchadnezzar's court.

—Paul Thigpen

Invocation delivered by Rev. George Tribou at the American zone finals of the Davis Cup tennis matches:

"Lord, grant to the referee, the linesmen, and the umpires sharpness of vision and fairness of judgment that they may see from the sides with the same clarity with which You will be watching from above."

GET OUT OF HELL FREE

FMC member Pastor Harry Brotzman, Jr., of Victory Assembly of God, Natchitoches, LA, passes out a calling card whose back side resembles a "Chance" card from the game of *Monopoly*. There is an illustration of a convict in stripes being kicked out of jail. The card declares: "GET OUT OF HELL FREE" and cites John 3:16: "For God so loved the world that He gave His only begotten Son, that whosoever believeth in Him should not perish, but have everlasting life."

"The vision of the angels works softly and peaceably, awakening joy and exultation in opposition to the turmoil into which demons throw the soul."
> —Athanasius (296 A.D.)
> early church theologian

A lawyer was overheard praying in church: "We respectively request, and entreat, that due and adequate provisions be made this day and the date hereinafter subscribed, for the organizing of such methods and allocations and distribution as may be deemed necessary to properly assure the reception by and for said petitioner of such quantities of baked cereal products as shall, in the judgment of the aforementioned parishioners, constitute a sufficient supply thereof."
Interpretation: "...give us this day our daily bread."
> —via George Goldtrap
> Madison, TN

"As I understand it, this is fairly common for Fourth of July marriages."
© 1995 Ed Sullivan

FMC member Burt Rosenberg, a Messianic Jewish comedian in Silver Spring, MD, travels around the country in a full-time comedy ministry to prisons and churches. It's called "Big Fun in the Spirit Ministries," and he says his mission is "to bring mirth to the earth."

"I think the same thing causes a person to come to Christ that causes a person to become a

"Now, boys, our camp director, Brother Blooper, will go over the camp rules."
© 1989 Dennis Daniel (*Brother Blooper*)

comedian," Burt says. "It's a sense of not quite belonging to this world. To laugh deeply requires *surrender*. You have to let go, give up control. And that also is the aim of faith. I use comedy not to help people escape reality, like other comedians do, but to find Reality."

A priest and a layman were watching a prize fight. When one of the fighters made the sign of the cross before the bell, the priest's companion said, "See that! He made the sign of the cross. Will that help him, father?"

"It will — if he knows how to box," the priest said.
—R. O. Brotherton
Our Sunday Visitor

"*JN's* article on Dr. Lloyd John Ogilvie, the newly elected U.S. Senate Chaplain, brought to mind a story that happened back in the 1970's. Lloyd was then minister of a Presbyterian Church in Bethlehem, PA, where a group of clergy met weekly to study the verses prescribed in the common

The inevitable finally occurred — a potluck with nothing but baked beans.
© 1995 Wendell W. Simons

lectionary for the following Sunday. Each would then prepare their own sermon, preaching on essentially the same passages.

"Lloyd was confronted after church by a woman who told him that she was sick and tired of hearing him preach about Jesus Christ, and that she was going elsewhere.

"Six months later, after the worship service in his church, Lloyd was confronted again by the same woman. This time she poked a bony finger into his chest and said, 'Darn you, I've been to every church in town, and they're all saying the same thing!' "

—Rev. Dr. Bob White
United Reform Churches of
Stockwell Green & Briston Hill
London, England

"If we tell the media, Papa, we'll lose our nice farm life, our privacy, our spiritual peace. Is it worth it, just for money from TV and magazines, book publishers, movie people... Papa... Papa?"
© 1993 Ed Sullivan

After the funeral of one of his parishioners, 94-year-old Hazel von Jeschki, Fr. John J. Fetterman, rector at Grace Episcopal Church in Madison, WI, noted in the church bulletin that she had left very specific handwritten instructions for her funeral service. The woman, who had never married, wrote: "There will be no male pallbearers. They wouldn't take me out when I was alive; I don't want them to take me out when I'm dead."

In an article expressing alarm that "16 percent of clergy are divorcing," *The Lutheran* reported that Bishop Wayne E. Weissenbuehler "recommends to clergy in the Rocky Mountain Synod that they buy a hot tub and spend at least 15 minutes with their spouse in it daily."

Philip Neri, a 16th-century Italian priest, always started his day with a prayer and this saying:
"A joke a day
"And I'm on my way,
"With no fear of tomorrow."

"*Church*: A place where you encounter nodding acquaintances."
—via Molli Mertel
Smithfield, VA

Atheist: "A person with no invisible means of support."
—Oscar Levant

"The board voted that, beginning next week, coffee hour will be before — not after — the church service."
© 1995 Wendell W. Simons

Preacher: a person who talks in someone else's sleep.

"A good sermon should have a good beginning and a good ending, and they should be as close together as possible."
—George Burns

"Few sinners are saved after the first 20 minutes of a sermon."
—Mark Twain

"So, for the most part, that'll be my sermon. What do you think the reaction to it will be?"
© 1994 Cartoons by Johns

Rev. Philip J. Anstedt of Sarasota, FL, a retired United
Church of Christ pastor, uses this calling card in retirement:

NO MONEY	NO JOB
NO WORRIES	NO PROSPECTS
NO CLOCKS	NO REPORTS

REV. PHILIP J. (PHIL) ANSTEDT
2596 Clubhouse Circle #101
Sarasota, Florida 34232
Tel.: 813-923-3710

GOLF BALLS SLICED   WILD STORIES SHARED

© 1993 Doc Goodwin (*Phillip's Flock*)

"After church one Sunday my six-year-old son asked if we
could go swimming that afternoon. I told him I couldn't take
him because I had to be at the church for a celebration
honoring our senior members. After a deafening pause, he
said, 'I guess I won't be one.' 'One what?' I asked. 'A
preacher,' he said. 'It's just too much work.'

"We went swimming Monday afternoon."

—Rev. Jeff Knighton
First Christian Church
Scott City, KS

"Make a joyful noise to the Lord all the lands."
—Psalms 100:1

A PRAYER FOR HUMOR AND LONGEVITY

Dear Lord:
Grant me faith;
grant me hope;
Let good humor
help me cope.
Let me spread the love
you give
And find a peaceful
way to live.
Use my talents;
Bless my daring
To show others
Christian caring.
Build my friendships,
Grace, and levity,
But — primarily —
Grant longevity.
                    —Shirley Vogeler Meister
                    Indianapolis, IN

~ Chapter 8 ~
August

Why don't ya just let God watch the game?

"Let me hear somebody say 'Amen.'"   "Amen!"

© 1990 Ed Koehler

In his book *It's Anybody's Ballgame*, Hall of Fame sports broadcaster Joe Garagiola has a chapter called "God in a Sweatshirt," raising some questions about which team God roots for when both sides pray to Him.

He tells this story about his friend Yogi Berra:

When he came up to bat, a baseball player noted for his piousness always marked a cross with his bat in the dirt next to home plate.

When he did this in a game against the New York Yankees, catcher Berra, also a religious man, reached over and rubbed out the cross with his catcher's mitt.

"Why don't ya just let God watch the game?" Berra said.

"Did I pray when I played? Yes, I think most players did, usually during the National Anthem," writes Garagiola, a former St. Louis Cardinals catcher. "For me, it was a time to meditate, a quiet moment when I could ask God to keep me from injury and let me do my best.

"I think most players today ask for the same things. I can easily understand how players, coaches, and fans occasionally let a prayer slip out for that base hit that'll win the World Series or a field goal that'll win the Super Bowl.

"But when it comes to a strikeout, an error, or a slump being God's will, then I think He's taking Yogi Berra's advice and just watching the game. I just can't believe with all the problems available to Him, God is worried about whether a baseball player strikes out or a football player catches a pass.

"Besides, if prayers really helped teams win, clubs like the Saints, the Cardinals, the Padres, and the Friars would have the edge. Take care of your own, right?"

Garagiola also thinks that God is more likely to be in the loser's locker room. "He's with those who are suffering, right?"

Pat Kelly, a free-swinging outfielder with the Baltimore Orioles several years ago, was married to a minister's daughter and always went to chapel before games.

One day, Kelly encountered his manager, Earl Weaver.

"Earl," Kelly said, "I feel great. I've just left the chapel, and once again I've learned to walk with the Lord."

"Too bad you didn't learn how to walk with the bases loaded," Weaver said.

"When's the last time you got down on your knees and prayed, Skip?" Kelly asked.

"The last time I sent you up to pinch hit," Weaver said.

—Joe Garagiola
It's Anybody's Ballgame

"It is said that it's hard for churches in Arizona to motivate people with thoughts of the future life, because it's so beautiful here in the winter that Heaven has no attraction. And in the summer it's so hot here that Hell doesn't scare them."

—Fred Sevier
Sun City, AZ

A boy who loved to go fishing with his dad was reciting the 23rd Psalm in Sunday School. When he got to the fourth verse, he said: "Thy rod and Thy reel, they comfort me."

—Dick Van Dyke

THE FAMILY CIRCUS

Christine M. Irvin of Columbus, OH, spotted this message on a church's outside sign during a heat wave in August: "COME WORSHIP IN PRAYER-CONDITIONED SANCTUARY."

"Anybody who has ever used the

"If summer had Christmas it would be perfect."

Reprinted with permission of Bil Keane

expression, 'It was no Sunday school picnic' has obviously never been to a Sunday school picnic."
—via Rev. Ronald H. Weinelt
St. John's Lutheran Church
Rincon, GA

Chronicling the story of a rebuilding project at First Congregational Church, Murphys, CA, the building committee chair reported to the congregation:
"It was discovered during the building program that the left side of the 90-year-old sanctuary actually extends five feet into the street. That means that those of you sitting on the left side of the building are actually sitting in the street. We have discovered a unique ministry here in Murphys. We have found out how to minister to street people without even leaving the church building."
—Rev. Jane Gibbons Huang
First Congregational Church
Murphys, CA

Sign seen on the front lawn of a church in Brentwood, CA: "FOR SALE BY OWNER."

Question: "What do you get if you cross a praying mantis with a termite?"
Answer: "An insect that says grace before he eats your house."

"When a Bible salesman was asked how he consistently sold more Bibles than anyone else, he replied: 'I jjjust aaasked eeeach ppprospect if he wwwanted to bbbuy a Bbbible, or hhhave me rrread it to hhhim.' "
—Jim Reed

Joyce Cary, the late English novelist, wrote a book about an artist titled *The Horse's Mouth*. In it, the painter, Gully Jimpson, is dying and is being attended by a very solemn nun.

Gully says to her: "Why don't you enjoy life, mother? I would be laughing all around my neck at this minute, if my shirt wasn't a bit on the tight side."

The nun replies, "It would be better for you to pray."

And Gully says, "Ah, 'tis the same thing, mother, 'tis the same thing."

—via Rev. Stuart A. Schlegel
Santa Cruz, CA

"Pride is the downward drag of all things into an easy solemnity. Seriousness is not a virtue. It would be heresy, but a much more sensible heresy, to say that seriousness is a vice. It is really a natural trend or lapse into taking one's self gravely, because it is the easiest thing to do. It is much easier to write a good *Times* leading article than a good joke in *Punch*. For solemnity flows out of men naturally; but laughter is a leap. It is easy to be heavy; hard to be light."

—G.K. Chesterton

ORIGINAL SIN

"As members of a grace-bearing institution, we could investigate whether taking oneself too seriously was part of the original sin. Adam and Eve were deceived by the promise that if they disobeyed, they should be as gods. If Adam and Eve had laughed at the snake, we'd still be on Easy Street. People are never more reasonable than when they are sincerely laughing."

—Fr. Robert F. Griffin, CSC, *Our Sunday Visitor*

Rev. Roland has a very small church.
© 1995 Steve Phelps

In some Christian theologies, the rapture is the bodily ascent of the saved into heaven just before Armageddon. A Pentecostal preacher assured his flock that they would be "the first to be taken up in the rapture because the Gospel declares 'The dead in Christ shall rise first.' "

"There is no beautifier of complexion, or form, or behavior, like the wish to scatter joy — and not pain — around us."
　　　　　　　　　　　　—Ralph Waldo Emerson

William Brower, associate director of speech at Princeton Theological Seminary, passed on this poem from his favorite poet, Robert Frost:

> *Forgive, O Lord*
> *My little jokes on Thee,*
> *And I'll forgive*
> *Thy great big one on me.*

FMC member Pastor Denny J. Brake of Raleigh, NC, observes that the reasons people give for not going to church also may be used as reasons for not going to bars.
"I stopped going to bars because...
"Every time I went there they asked for money."
"The bartender was the only one who spoke to me."
"Some of the people who go there are hypocrites."
"They don't sing the kind of songs I like."
"My dad made me go with him when I was a kid."
"You don't have to go to bars to be inebriated."

The English poet Samuel Taylor Coleridge (1772-1834) was entertaining a visitor one day when the conversation turned to children. "I believe," said the visitor, "that children should be given a free rein to think and act, and thus learn at an early age to make their own decisions. This is the only way they can grow into their full potential."
"I would like you to see my flower garden," Coleridge interrupted his visitor, and he led the man outside. The

visitor took one look and exclaimed, "Why, this is nothing but a yard full of weeds!"

"It used to be filled with roses," said Coleridge, "but this year I thought I would let the garden grow as it willed without my tending to it. This is the result."

—*Apple Seeds*
via Rev. Brian Cavanaugh

"The people who hanged Christ never, to do them justice, accused Him of being a bore — on the contrary, they thought Him too dynamic to be safe. It has been left for later generations to muffle up that shattering personality and surround Him with an atmosphere of tedium. We have very efficiently pared the claws of the Lion of Judah, certified Him 'meek and mild,' and recommended Him as a fitting household pet for pale curates and pious old ladies."

—Dorothy L. Sayers

When he was pastor of Zion Lutheran Church in Doylestown, OH, Rev. Paul Lintern started a comedy club called "Saturday Night Alive" in his church social hall. A parishioner played music on an electronic keyboard. A troupe of singers led the audience in a variety of songs. Actors put on skits. And Lintern warmed up the audience with jokes — for instance, this David Letterman take-off on "The Top 10 Things People Think about while Singing a Hymn":

10. The pot roast.
9. What does pastor wear under robes?
8. Will the person behind me ever hit the right note?
7. 90 minutes till kickoff.
6. Did I turn off the curling iron?
5. The likelihood of the ceiling fan falling and hitting me on the head.
4. How many people have lost more hair than I have?
3. How would the hymn sound if Metallica played it?
2. Are there doughnuts at fellowship?
1. How many more verses?

This well-attended comedy club always ended with a celebrative worship service and a buffet.

A GIFT OF HUMOR

"As your moderator this year, let me offer you a gift of good humor. I encourage all committee moderators to begin each meeting with prayer and good humor, a kind-hearted joke, a happy story, something which will make us smile after we say 'Amen.' You may also wish to include some of this good humor in your reports to Presbytery.

"The best evangelism in the world is laughter, a church laughing — not naive tittering, not sarcastic boisterousness, not angry irony, but deep, joyful laughter from the pit of our being...laughter which has suffered from the consequences of evil choices and found redemption and newness of life through the cross of Jesus Christ, laughter which remembers tears, yet knows beyond a shadow of a doubt that we are not to fear, for Jesus, God's good-humored Christ, has overcome the world before us."

—Rev. Sylvia C. Guinn-Ammons
at her installation as moderator
of the Presbytery of Denver, CO

"Men, women and children, who cannot live on gravity alone, need something to satisfy their lighter moods and hours, and he who ministers to this want is in a business established by the Author of our nature. If he worthily fulfills his mission, and amuses without corrupting, he need never feel that he has lived in vain."

—P.T. Barnum

"There's always a heated debate whenever Methodists do anything. As one commentator observed, 'Methodist preachers are like manure. Spread them around the state and they do a lot of good. Pile them together in one place and they get to stinking.' "

—Rev. William H. Willimon
Methodist minister

JN consulting editor Dennis Daniel, pastor of the First Southern Baptist Church in Payson, AZ, and creator of the *Brother Blooper* cartoons, writes:

"Pastors have more exposure to heartache and heartbreak than any other profession. And if we are not careful, we can become caught up in the gloom and doom, and miss out on the joy of our salvation. The same God who created tear ducts also created the funny bone. God has created us with a sense of humor to enable us to see above the clouds. And, believe me, there is no place funnier than a church. I have often been asked where I get my ideas for my *Brother Blooper* cartoons. I just keep my ears and eyes open around the church."

"Jewish spirituality has always found a place for humor. It has not forgotten that the Biblical God is a God of unexpected turns, twists, and surprises. God plays; God teases! Jewish spirituality loves the

Bro. BLOOPER

"The nominating committee has a concern that you might use this as an excuse to quit working with our youth."
© 1989 Dennis Daniel (*Brother Blooper*)

humor of a laughing insight into religion. Even the classics — the Talmud, the Zohar, the Hasidic stories — revel in the humorous tidbit: 'If one man calls you an ass, ignore it. If two or three call you an ass, start looking for a saddle.' "

—Matthias Newman, OSB
America

"When the missionaries first came to Africa, they had the Bible and we had the land. They said, 'Let us pray.' We closed our eyes. When we opened them, the tables had been turned: We had the Bible and they had the land."

—Bishop Desmond Tutu
South Africa

From "Plain English for Lawyers" by Richard C. Wydick, writing in the *California Law Review*:
"To grip and move your reader's mind, use concrete words, not abstractions. To see the difference, suppose that Moses' plagues on Egypt had been described in the language of a modern environmental report:

EXODUS 8:7

"As the Lord commanded...He lifted up the rod and smote the waters of the river...and all the waters that were in the river were turned to blood. And the fish that were in the river died; and the river stank, and the Egyptians could not drink the waters of the river; and there was blood throughout all the land of Egypt."

ALTERED VERSION

"In accordance with the directive theretofore received from higher authority, He caused the implement to come into contact with the water, whereupon a polluting effect was perceived. The consequent toxification reduced the conditions necessary for the sustenance of the indigenous population of the aquatic vertebrates below the level of continued viability. Olfactory discomfort standards were substantially exceeded, and potability declined. Social, economic and political disorientation was experienced to an unprecedented degree."
—via Steve Feldman
Jefferson City, MO

Comedian Steve Allen sent the following story to *JN*:
During an ecumenical gathering, someone rushed in shouting, "The building is on fire!"
* The Methodists at once gathered in a corner and prayed.
* The Baptists cried, "Everybody into the water."
* The Lutherans posted a notice on the door declaring

fire was evil, because it was the natural abode of the devil.

* The Congregationalists shouted, "Every man for himself!"
* The Seventh-Day Adventists proclaimed, "It's the vengeance of an angry God!"
* The Christian Scientists agreed among themselves that there really was not a fire.
* The Presbyterians appointed a chairperson, who was to appoint a committee to look into the matter and make a written report to the next session.
* The Episcopalians formed a procession and marched out in good order.
* The Unitarian-Universalists concluded that the fire had as much right to be there as anyone else.
* The Catholics passed a collection plate to cover the damages.

"Since my early days, I've known that the raw material of most comedy is painful. After all, what are jokes about? They're about how dumb people are, how drunk they were last night, how broke they are, how sexually frustrated, greedy or lazy… To refer to the Christian moral tradition, jokes are about the seven deadly sins: pride, convetousness, lust, anger, gluttony, envy, and sloth… The element of humor is necessary to human beings, necessary for the maintenance of sanity."
    —Steve Allen
    How to Be Funny

FMC member Bonnie Habbersett of Livonia, MI, passed on this chain letter, titled "The Perfect Pastor," which came to her anonymously with the request that she pass it on:

"Bless me, Father, for I have sinned. It has been 30 years since my last confession."

© 1990 M. Larry Zanco

"The results of a computerized survey indicate the perfect pastor preaches exactly 15 minutes. S/He condemns sin but never upsets anyone. S/He works from 8 a.m. until midnight and is also a janitor. S/He makes $50 a week, wears good clothes, buys good books, drives a good car, and gives about $50 weekly to the poor. S/He is 28 years old and has been preaching 30 years. S/He has a burning desire to work with teen-agers and spends all of his/her time with senior citizens. The perfect pastor smiles all the time with a straight face because s/he has a sense of humor that keeps him/her seriously dedicated to his/her work. S/He make 15 calls daily on parish families, shut-ins, and the hospitalized. S/He spends all of his/her time evangelizing the unchurched and is always in his/her office when needed. If your pastor does not measure up, simply send this letter to six other parishes that are tired of their pastor, too. Then bundle up your pastor and send him/her to the church at the top of the list. In one week, you will receive 1,643 pastors and one of them should be perfect. Have faith in this letter. One church broke the chain and got its old pastor back in less than three weeks."

"You want to make God laugh? Tell him your plans."
—John Chancellor

THE FAMILY CIRCUS

"What did Grace do that made her so amazing?"

Reprinted with permission of Bil Keane

OUT OF THE MOUTHS OF BABES

A family was staying overnight at a friend's home in another town. At bedtime, a little girl told her mother that she was afraid to sleep alone in a different bedroom.

The mother assured the girl that God and her guardian angel would watch over her while she was asleep.

The girl replied: "Yeah, but I want someone with skin on them to sleep with me."

Rev. Eldred Johnston, rector emeritus of St. Mark's Episcopal Church, Columbus, OH, writes that a little girl in his confirmation class went home and reported to her mother that the pastor had urged the children "to be kind to strangers because you never know, you might be entertaining angels in their underwear."

A mother took her small son to a Catholic church one Sunday morning. As the mass went on and on, he became restless. She tried, in vain, to assure the little boy that the mass would soon be over. Finally, he pointed to the tabernacle votive light — a candle in a red glass container that always stays lit — and asked: "Are we going to have to stay here until that red light turns green?"

—via Fr. Norman J. Muckerman
Liguori, MO

Arriving at the Gouldsboro (PA) United Methodist Church one Sunday morning, Rev. Timothy W. Ehrlich, the pastor, whispered to his six-year-old son, Shawn: "This is God's house. You must behave in it."

"Daddy," Shawn replied, "can I use God's bathroom?"

Joan Turner of Middletown, RI, recalls that she was at the beach with her children when her four-year-old son ran up to her, grabbed her hand, and led her to the shore, where a sea gull lay dead in the sand.

"Mommy, what happened to him?" the little boy asked.

"He died and went to heaven," the mother replied.

The boy thought a moment and then said: "And God threw him back down?"

FMC member Rev. Paul J. Davis, editor of *The Desert Wind*, newsletter of St. Anthony on the Desert Episcopal Church, Scottsdale, AZ, passes on the following item from the August issue:
"Our Newcomer Committee spent part of their time at their last meeting spraying ants in West Hall. Fr. Hal Daniell began the meeting by saying, 'Let us spray.' "

When FMC member Rev. Robert M. Ross, rector of Saint Peter's Episcopal Church, Osterville, MA, arrived at seminary, he noticed that someone had put up on the bulletin board a small sign with the simple message: "Job 7:11."
Supposing that it was a scriptural word of encouragement for seminarians, similar to John 3:16, Ross noted the citation and went home to look it up. It read: "Therefore I will not restrain my mouth; I will speak in the anguish of my spirit; I will complain in the bitterness of my soul." (NRSV)
How awful this person must be suffering! Ross thought, wondering if the sign was a cry for help. The next day he took his concerns to the chaplain.
"Oh, that was on the employment board," the chaplain smiled. "There's a job opening at the Seven-Eleven."

BULLETIN BLOOPERS THAT GNASH THE TEETH
From the bulletin of St. Leo Catholic Church, Howland, ME: "Parish Council meetings are held the first Monday of the month after the Wednesday evening Mass."
—via Rev. André L. Houle, OMI

From the church bulletin of St. Francis de Sales Church, Albany, NY: "Wednesday, May 9, is Ascension Thursday."
—via Kathleen Shea
Haworth, NJ

From the bulletin of the First United Methodist Church, New Kensington, PA: "OFFERTORY ANTHEM: 'Be Not Afraid' — Cancel Choir"
—via Rev. Joseph A. Hajdu

"In the church newsletter, our chairman of Christian education expressed concern about the Sunday school students, who were arriving late every morning, as follows: 'When the opening is delayed due to stranglers, it cuts into the time that teachers have to spend with your children sharing God's word.' "
—Rev. Dann J. Ettner
Atwater, CA

From the bulletin of Peace Lutheran Church, Manhattan, KS: "Before the lecture he will be discussing his personal faith struggle in suffering at a potluck supper."

James L. Sullivan recalled that, when he was president of a Baptist publishing house, the printing of a Sunday school lesson was halted when the title, "Paul Pleads for a Slave" was printed as "Paul Pleads for a Shave."
—*Ohio Baptist Messenger*

The caption beneath a photograph of the St. Olaf College choir in the *Sun Cities (AZ) Independent* described the choir as "internationally renounced."

Ed Golder, religion editor of the *Grand Rapids (MI) Press*, went to the library of Calvin College and searched for references to "Humor and Christianity." He found only five.

"I think I just found the perfect church... now if I can only keep it a secret."
© 1994 Jonny Hawkins

Shortly afterwards, however, David Stanley of Kennesaw, GA, wrote *JN* that while reading the Institutes of the Christian Religion III: 19:9, he unearthed the following quote from John Calvin (1509-1564):
"We are nowhere forbidden to laugh, or to be satisfied with food, ...or to be delighted with music, or to drink wine."

And Pastor R. Vernon Babcock of Hunter Community Church, Franklin, OH, passed on this quote from John Calvin:
"There is not one blade of grass, there is no color in this world that is not intended to make us rejoice."

"Sure our church is reaching out — about as far from here as we can get!"
© 1992 Ed Koehler

"Christ came to bring joy: joy to children, joy to parents, joy to families and to friends, joy to workers and to scholars, joy to the sick and joy to the elderly, joy to all humanity. In a true sense, joy is the keynote of the Christian message and the recurring motif of the Gospels... Be messengers of joy."
—Pope John Paul II
The Times of the Spirit

"Do you want to know one of the best ways to win over people and lead them to God? It consists in giving them joy and making them happy."
—St. Francis of Assisi

"The fullness of joy is to behold God in everything."
            —Dame Julian of Norwich

After the death of the great 18th-century Methodist evangelist, George Whitefield, a New York woman commented: "Mr. Whitefield was so cheerful that it tempted me to become a Christian."

FMC member Donald Prout, pastor of Rosanna Christian Church in Reservoir, Victoria, Australia, researched the books, sermons, and biographies of the famous English Baptist preacher, Charles Haddon Spurgeon (1834-1892) and discovered a treasury of wit and humor.

Spurgeon once advised young preachers: "The horrors are a poor bait. The world will never be converted to God until Christians cry less and laugh and sing more."

Recalling a series of dull lectures by another preacher on Paul's Epistle to the Hebrews, Spurgeon commented: "Paul, in that Epistle, exhorts us to *suffer* the word of exhortation, and we did so."

Reviewing a book on Daniel by another preacher, Spurgeon wrote: "This learned book is enough to perplex and distract any ordinary mortal. We had sooner read a table of logarithms."

A woman who had "the reputation of being a regular virago" once cornered Spurgeon and gave him a lengthy tongue-lashing.

Spurgeon smiled and said: "Yes, thank you; I am quite well. I hope you are the same."

The woman persisted in villifying him. Still smiling, Spurgeon replied: "Yes, it does look rather as if it is going to rain; I think I had better be getting on."

"Bless the man!" the woman exclaimed, "he's as deaf as a post; what's the use storming at him?"

When Dr. Theodore Cuyler and Spurgeon were walking one day in the woods, Spurgeon suddenly stopped and said: "Come, Theodore, let us thank God for laughter."

YE ARE THE HOLY WITS OF THE EARTH

The Apostle Paul seems to have suggested to the early Christians that when evangelizing, they use humor in witnessing.

Writing to the Colossians, Paul advises: "Let your speech always be gracious, seasoned with salt, so that you may know how you ought to answer everyone." (Col. 4:6 RSV)

The New Jerusalem Bible translates this passage: "Talk to them agreeably and with a flavor of wit, and try to fit your answers to the needs of each one."

Rev. Michael Northrop of the Comstock (MI) Church of the Nazarene passes on this passage from the book *Word Meanings in the New Testament* by Ralph Earl:

"In the Greek comic writers, the verb *artyo* — 'season' — referred to the seasoning with the salt of wit. But too often this degenerated into off-color jokes."

Paul seems to be calling Christians to a higher, holier level of wit and humor that will not only capture people's attention but teach them the truths of the Gospel.

Paul may have been asking the early Christians to imitate the wit, holy humor, and good cheer of Jesus.

If that is so, then Jesus' words to His followers — "Ye are the salt of the earth." (Matt: 5-13 KJV) — take on another dimension of meaning: "You are the holy wits of the earth."

—Cal Samra
Editor, *The Joyful Noiseletter*

CLEAN COMEDIANS

"It doesn't have to be filthy to be funny." That's the motto of the Clean Comedians, a group of comedians in the Los Angeles area founded by FMC member Adam Christing. Adam, a talented comedian-

"I really regret you're moving, Mr. Thigpen. You've been excellent material for sermons."
© 1991 Goddard Sherman

magician who lives in La Mirada, CA, books engagements for his group of Clean Comedians with businesses and churches. He's a member of Grace Evangelical Free Church in La Mirada.

Even in his most profound works, G.K. Chesterton, the great English Catholic defender of Christianity, was so amusing a writer that his more solemn critics actually rebuked him for levity.

Chesterton, who had a great influence on C.S. Lewis, once was moved to defend himself as follows: "Whether a man chooses to tell the truth in long sentences or in short jokes is a problem analogous to whether he chooses to tell the truth in French or in German."

"It's not easy to be joyful during hard times," writes FMC playshop leader John J. Boucher of Hicksville, NY, a Catholic charismatic and author of a book called *Is Talking to God a Long-Distance Call?*

"My wife Therese and I have five children, and often I get frustrated, angry, and depressed over our family's financial situation. It seems the only ones who can make a deposit on a new car are the pigeons.

"Circumstances suck joy out of me. I can easily get down on myself and even on God. With St. Teresa of Avila, I lament, 'Lord, if this is the way you treat your friends, no wonder you have so few of them!'

"At times like these, I believe the Lord is saying to us: 'Rejoice in the Lord — *today*!' 'Rejoice in the Lord always. I shall say it again: rejoice.'(Phil. 4:4).

"One of the most joyful people I've ever met was a Native American woman from Arizona. She grew up in a large and terribly poor family. Still, they shared everything they had with their friends and neighbors. When they were down to their last five dollars, her father would always say: 'Let's have a party!' He'd spend that five dollars on ice cream and invite all the neighbors to come over. By God's grace, her family always had all that they needed.

"Even in the pits of depression, we, too, can throw a party. We are the children of a loving God! We can rejoice in the sure hope that God will get us through any trial or tribulation.

"Joy is a decision. We need to decide to rejoice *today*, whatever our circumstances or feelings.

★ Ask the Lord to release the Spirit of Joy within you.

★ Decide to do things that are rejoicing (i.e. have a party, give gifts, dance, sing, etc.).

★ Be persistent.

★ Make the following the foundation stone of your growth in Christian joy: personal daily prayer, repentance, friendships, service to others, leisure, play, and a sense of humor."

JN consulting editor Malcolm Muggeridge said he always derived great comfort from these lines from the English poet William Blake (1827):

> *Joy and woe are woven fine,*
> *A clothing for the soul divine,*
> *Under every grief and pine*
> *Runs a joy with silken twine.*
> *It is right it should be so;*
> *Man was made for joy and woe;*
> *And when this we rightly know,*
> *Through the world we safely go.*

"God cannot endure that unfestive, mirthless attitude of ours in which we eat our bread in sorrow, with pretentious, busy haste, or even with shame. Through our daily meals He is calling us to rejoice, to keep holiday in the midst of our working day."

> —Dietrich Bonhoeffer
> Lutheran pastor executed
> by the Nazis for his
> opposition to Hitler

"Cool it with the spiritual joy, Brother."
© 1987 Ed Sullivan (*The Gift of Laughter*)

"May the God of hope bring you such joy and peace in your faith that the power of the Holy Spirit will remove all bounds to hope."
—Romans 15:13

A PRAYER FOR COURAGE AND JOY
"*Lord, give us grace and strength to persevere. Give us courage and joy and the quiet mind.*"
—Robert Louis Stevenson

~ Chapter 9 ~
September

How to use humor
to pry away the bucks

"Try to give more than your usual dollar, Harry."

FUND-RAISING IDEA OF THE YEAR

Μψ λιφε φλοωσ ον ιν ενδλεσσ σονγ αβοῶε εαρτη϶σ λαμεντατιον. Ι ηεαρ τηε ρεαλ τηουγη϶ φαρ–οφφ ηψμν τηατ ηαιλσ α νεω χρεατιον. Τηρουγη αλλ τηε τυμυλτ ανδ τηε στριφε Ι ηεαρ τηατ μυσιχ ρινγινγ. Ιτ σουνδσ αν εχηο ιν μψ σουλ. Ηοω χαν Ι κεεπ φρομ σινγινγ Αμεριχα϶σ ηεαλτη χαρε χρισισ.

Thus began a fund-raising letter we received from Hunter "Patch" Adams, M.D., executive director, on behalf of a building program for the Gesundheit! Institute in Arlington, VA. The two-page letter was entirely in Greek.

Dr. Adams, an FMC member who is known as "the clown prince of physicians," later explained that he "gets so many fund-raising letters that they all start to look the same and they might as well be in Greek." So he decided to send a letter out in Greek.

Result: "We've had a great response," Dr. Adams reported. "And the donations are still coming in."

The Gesundheit! Institute bills itself as a place "where good health is a laughing matter." Its literature features this quotation from the 17th-century English physician Dr. Thomas Sydenham: "The arrival of a good clown exercises more beneficial influence upon the health of a town than of 20 jackasses laden with drugs."

The preacher was trying to get his people to be more enthusiastic about their church, so he said in his sermon:

"If this church is going to get anywhere, it has to learn to crawl."

And the people said, "Let it crawl, Rev., let it crawl!"

Then he said, "And after it learns to crawl, it has to learn to walk."

And the people said, "Let it walk, Rev., let it walk!"

Then he got excited and said, "After this church learns to walk, it has to learn to run!"

And finally he said, "And if this church is going to run, it's going to take *money*!"

And the people said, "Let it *crawl*, Rev., let it *crawl*!"

—Flip Wilson

A pastor was talking to the church organist. "When I finish my sermon," he said, "I'll ask for all those in the congregation who want to contribute $400 toward the church's mortgage to stand up. In the meantime, you can provide appropriate music."

"Any suggestions?" the organist asked.

"You might try 'The Star-Spangled Banner,' " the pastor replied.

During an examination, a rookie police officer was asked what strategy he would use to disperse a threatening crowd.

"I would take up a collection," he wrote.

—via Catherine Hall
Pittsburgh, PA

Columnist James J. Kilpatrick writes that "a truly clever pun is a work of art in a class by itself." He cited this classic pun:

"The pastor of a Lutheran church in Philadelphia decided to go easy on low-income members of his congregation. The Rev. Glenn Zorb recognized 'that not everyone is fit to be tithed.' "

THE FAMILY CIRCUS

"Are you and Daddy OK for money?"

Reprinted with permission of Bil Keane

"When we eat out, most of us expect to tip the waiter or waitress 15 percent. When we suggest 10 percent as a minimum church offering, some folks are aghast. Think about it. Better yet, pray about it."
—via Rev. Felix A. Lorenz Jr.
Northville, MI

Bumper sticker seen on the van of Msgr. Joseph P. Dooley, pastor of St. Rocco's Church, Martins Creek, PA:
IF YOU LOVE JESUS, TITHE!
ANYONE CAN HONK!

"I want to tithe," a man told his pastor. "I want to give 10 percent of my income to my church. When my income was $50 a week, I gave $5 to the church every Sunday. When I was successful in business and my weekly income rose to $500 a week, I gave $50 to my church every Sunday. But now my income has gone to $5,000 a week, and I just can't bring myself to give $500 to the church every week."
The pastor said, "Why don't we pray over this?" The pastor began to pray, "Dear God, please make this man's weekly income $500 a week so that he can tithe..."
—Rev. John L. Mand
St. John's Episcopal Church
Dryden, MI

"You can do it, fella...you can open those fingers and let the money go! Try it...try! That's it...great! They're moving..."
© 1990 Ed Sullivan

STEWARDSHIP ACCORDING TO COMEDIAN TOMMY DINARDO

From *The Best of Tommy DiNardo*:

"One of my favorite stories in the Bible is the story of Ananias and his wife Sapphira in Acts 5. The early Christians shared everything. But Ananias and Sapphira sold a piece of property and held back some of the money for themselves instead of giving it all to Peter for the community.

"After Peter upbraided them for lying, they both fell down and breathed their last.

"Everybody saw this, so I'm thinking there must have been a heck of a collection the next Sunday in church.

"How many people look to see how much the person next to them is putting in the collection plate? There's a definite technique to this. You just don't look straight at it. You just sort of glance out of the corner of your eye.

"When the plate passes them, there are some people who don't see anything at all. They act as though they don't even see the basket go by.

"This is where ushers should come into play. Put a little pressure on the cheapskates.

"When I was a little lad in church, the ushers had these collection baskets with long poles. They were more intimidating than the baskets you just let people pass around. With that long pole, you can slide that puppy in there, and if the guy is not looking, you stop right in front of his face — and wiggle the change a little bit. And if he still isn't looking, you just hit him in the chest."

"We can remember George as a convicted counterfeiter or as an unselfish and generous individual who paid off the church deficit."
© 1993 M. Larry Zanco

A notorious gambler offered to donate $1,000 to a church project for the homeless. The offer greatly upset a church elder. She confronted the pastor: "We can't take his money. It's the devil's money."

"If that's the case," the pastor replied calmly, "the devil has had his hands on it long enough. Now let's see what God can do with it."

"A British recluse named Ernest Digweed died in the early 1980's and left the equivalent of $57,000 in his will for Jesus Christ if he should return to earth before the end of the 20th century. Digweed's heirs asked the courts to invalidate the will and divide the money among them. The judges agreed but they took out insurance with Lloyds of London for the amount just in case Christ does return within Digweed's stipulated time."

—William J. Freburger

Thomas Cook, treasurer of St. Michael's Episcopal Church, Orlando, FL, decided to use humor in a letter to parishioners to remind them to keep their pledges current. He wrote: "Here are the 10 worst things that can happen when we are behind in pledges:

10. Church won't have money to buy wine for communion.
9. George (Rev. Dr. George M. Gann, rector) will have to cut back on cigarettes.
8. We'll have to turn the air conditioner off during church services.
7. Can't pay child care givers; you'll have to take turns in the nursery.
6. Can't buy batteries for the church microphone (think anyone will notice?).
5. No more coffee at coffee hour; we'll have to call it water hour.
4. No more paper for pledge letters; it will come on a postcard and your mail-carrier will read it!
3. In order to save on postage, we will be recruiting you to hand-deliver the *St. Michael's Messenger*.

2. As a cost-cutting measure, the organ will be turned off and Andrew, our organist, will use a harmonica.

1. I'll have to write another letter and it won't be as humorous as this one."

Grace Episcopal Church of Jefferson City, MO, hosted its second annual "No Excuse Sunday," with the following props provided to anticipate any excuse for not attending church:

"Blankets and sweaters for those who don't come because the church is too cold; fans for those who stay away because it is too warm; hard hats for those who are afraid the roof will fall in; stop-watches and whistles for those who think the sermons are too long; cushions for those who think the pews are too hard; and name tags for those who are afraid they won't be recognized."

The church also announced it would provide free transportation.

—via Frank W. Way
Jefferson City, MO

"Mirth is like a flash of lightning that breaks through a gloom of clouds and glitters for the moment. Cheerfulness keeps up a daylight in the mind, filling it with steady and perpetual serenity."

—Samuel Johnson

Mark Twain once attended a church service where a missionary appealed for funds to evangelize the heathen in a foreign land.

"After 10 minutes of a description about their unhappy plight, I wanted to give $50," Twain wrote. "The preacher kept on another 15 minutes and that gave me time to realize that $50 was an extravagance, so I cut it in half. At the end of another 10 minutes, I had reduced it to $5. When at the end of an hour of speaking the plates were finally passed, I was so annoyed that I reached in and helped myself to a quarter."

A woman was married to a miserly man. She had to fight for everything she got. One day, she told him she was going window shopping. He said, "Look, but don't buy."

A few hours later, she came home with a new dress. "What is this?" her husband fumed. "I thought I told you to look but not buy."

"Well," she explained, "I saw this lovely dress and thought I'd try it on, and when I did the devil said, 'It sure looks good on you.' "

"Right then you should have told him, 'Get thee behind me, Satan,' " her husband exclaimed.

"I did," she answered, "but when he got behind me he said, 'It sure looks good from the back, too.' "

—Rev. Bernard Brunsting
Funny Things Happen

On the wall of the men's room at a Kansas truck stop were scribbled the words: "If God be for us, who can be against us?"

Scrawled beneath someone had added: "The highway patrol!"

—Msgr. Arthur Tonne
Jokes Priests Can Tell

Even a dummy can teach good stewardship. Rev. Roy P. White, pastor of Epworth United Methodist Church in Norfolk, VA, uses a ventriloquist's dummy named Isaac ("God's laugh" in Hebrew) to teach stewardship, among other things, to children and adults.

Isaac, a Charlie McCarthy look-alike, says "a lot of outrageous things that parishioners laugh at, but they'd get mad at me if I said them," White said. "Some people think they get a better sermon when the dummy preaches."

Sample dialogue:

WHITE: "Well, Isaac, I've decided to raise your weekly allowance from $1 to $1.25. What are you going to give to the church?"·

ISAAC: "Nothing. Why would I give money to the church?"

WHITE: "It's important to give something to God."

ISAAC: "Why? God doesn't need money. If God wants money, He just looks down and says, 'Give me money!'"

WHITE: "God wants us to share."

ISAAC: "Okay, I'll give two cents a week."

WILL ROGERS NEVER MET A PREACHER HE DIDN'T LIKE

The great American humorist Will Rogers wrote down his thoughts about a conference of pastors he attended in Indianapolis during the Depression in the early 1930's:

"At this conference of ministers, my friend Will Hays made quite an impassioned speech in favor of a drive to raise a Pension Fund for Preachers. Now that is a real Cause. The ministry in all denominations are the poorest paid workers in the world.

"They could form a union and demand more pay, but they don't get enough to pay dues into a union, so they can't form one. They can't demand regular hours for they don't know what hour some of their constituents may need a christening or a wedding ceremony. They have to be respectable, and the high cost of living advance is nothing in comparison to the high cost of respectability. Why, I can't remember when a man could be considered respectable without belonging to a golf club.

"I preached one time in a church in Cleveland, but the collection didn't warrant me carrying it on as a steady profession. Preaching should not only be done by a preacher, but by a man like Mahatma Gandhi, who can do fasting when necessary, for it will be necessary."

Rogers wrote to another minister friend:
"Love to all your congregation, including the ones that are not paid up. It's just hard times. They mean well, parson. They got just as much religion as the paid-up ones. So you will just have to trust 'em, and give 'em a little preaching 'on time.'

"You see, preaching is one of the few things that folks have never been able to dope out exactly what it's worth, anyhow. Some preachers ought to pay admission to get into church themselves, but as a rule, preachers do a mighty good job, and are underpaid.

"There is a lot of dignity about the clerical profession that you would have to work years for in any other line. You are sympathetic, useful, instructive, and the most worthwhile profession ever invented."

Sign posted on a hospital ward, via Leslie Gibson, RN, of Dunedin, FL:

> **NOTICE**
>
> DUE TO THE CURRENT
> BUDGET CUTBACKS,
> THE LIGHT AT THE
> END OF THE TUNNEL
> WILL BE TURNED OFF
> UNTIL FURTHER NOTICE

FMC member Bishop Mar Aprem, head of the ancient Chaldean Orthodox Church of the East in Kerala, India, has been tickling the funny bones of Christians, Moslems, and Hindus with his collection of down-home jokes. Here's a sampling from a collection the bishop self-published:

"When a member of a church in India won a lottery worth 100,000

Budget crunch brings out new techniques in the Chapel by the Sea ushers.
© 1995 Steve Phelps

rupees, his wife went to the bishop and told him that she was afraid to tell this glad news to her husband because he had a heart problem and any sudden excitement could cause a heart attack.

"The bishop offered to break the news gently to her husband. He visited the house and asked the man, 'Wouldn't it be a good thing if you won 1,000 rupees in the lottery?' The man replied that he still would have to work to support his family.

" 'What about 10,000 rupees?' the bishop asked. This did not excite the man, so the bishop carefully raised the amount to 50,000 and finally to 100,000 rupees.

" 'If I got 100,000 rupees, I would give half of it to you, your Excellency,' the man replied.

"The bishop had a heart attack, and the man called an ambulance."

"Stewardship is more than setting up soup kitchens and overnight shelters. It is good and right that we reach into the river of despair and rescue people who are drowning. But it is time to move upstream and see who's throwing them in."
—Bishop Edmond Browning
Episcopal Diocese of Montana

Rev. Graydon H. Pittman, pastor-emeritus of the First United Methodist Church, Emporia, KS, writes: "When I see a man go to sleep in church, I thank God that he at least has the ability to relax." Rev. Pittman says he was impressed when he received the following

"The collection nearly doubles when Berkoski ushers."
© 1992 Goddard Sherman

advice from Dr. R. W. Wood of Johns Hopkins University: "Be careful to appreciate the people who go to sleep when

you are speaking. You may be
helping more than you know.
For several years, I've been
going to London to lecture
before the Royal Society. At
the lectures, there was an old
fellow who invariably fell
asleep. The last time I spoke
his place was vacant. A
gentleman said, 'He died
recently and left the Society
$150,000. He explained in his
will that he was troubled with
insomnia and it was only in

"In just a moment I'll pronounce you
man and wife. But first a word about
our fund drive for a new organ."
© 1992 Goddard Sherman

the meetings of the Royal Society that he could sleep, so he
desired to show his appreciation by the legacy.' "

SPOONERISMS

An Anglican clergyman, the Rev. William Archibald
Spooner (1844-1930) is regarded as the all-time champion of
the verbal blooper. Spooner, the warden of New College in
Oxford, England, gave his name to a form of crazy talk
known as "spoonerisms."

A spoonerism is an unintentional interchange of sounds in
two or more words.

For instance, Rev. Spooner once told a rector: "The vicar
knows every crook and nanny in the parish."

One Sunday morning, Spooner told his congregation: "Let
us sing, 'The Kinkering Congs Their Tattles Tike.' " The
hymn was: "The Conquering Kings Their Titles Take."

On another occasion, he announced the next hymn would
be "From Iceland's Greasy Mountains." At a wedding, he
told the groom, "It is kistomary to cuss the bride."

In those days, pews were rented by members of Spooner's
Anglican congregation. One Sunday morning, Spooner told
a woman: "Madam, you are occupewing the wrong pie. Let
me sew you to your sheet."

Spooner, who taught history at Oxford, England, once said

to one of his nonproductive students: "You have hissed all your mystery lectures and have completely tasted two whole worms."

Spooner once preached sympathetically about a man who "had received a blushing crow." He meant to say "crushing blow."

He once preached about "the tearful chidings of the Gospel." He meant "cheerful tidings."

He once observed that, "although people differ in rank and station, at death they are all brought to a red devil." He meant to say "dead level."

At a gathering of members of Parliament, Spooner invited the M.P.s to give "three cheers for the queer old dean." He meant to say "the dear old queen," referring to Queen Victoria.

Calling on the dean of Christ Church, he asked the secretary, "Is the bean dizzy?" Giving the eulogy at a clergyman's funeral, he praised his departed colleague as a "shoving leopard to his flock."

In another sermon, he warned his congregation: "There is no peace in a home where a dinner swells." He intended to say "where a sinner dwells."

Speaking to a group of farmers, Spooner intended to greet them as "sons of toil," but said "I see before me tons of soil."

A young Presbyterian minister was called, upon short notice, to officiate at the parish church at Crathie, England, in the presence of Queen Victoria. The nervous minister was so overwhelmed by the majesty of the occasion that he blurted out the following prayer: "Grant that as Her Majesty grows to be an old woman she may be made a new man; and that in all righteous causes she may go forth before her people like a he-goat on the mountains."

A large denominational gathering in the Midwest heard a keynote speaker begin his message as follows: "Puke and weany men that we are... I mean, weak and puny men..."
—Tal Bonham

A pastor bowed his head and solemnly declared: "Let us pray for those who are sick of this congregation."
—George Goldtrap

IRONY IN THE ABBEY

"I pursued my walk to an arched door opening to the interior of the (Westminster) Abbey. The spaciousness and gloom of this vast edifice produce a profound and mysterious awe. We step cautiously and softly about, as if fearful of disturbing the hallowed silence of the tomb; while every footfall whispers along the walls, and chatters among the sepulchers...

"It seems as if the nature of the place presses down upon the soul, and hushes the beholder into noiseless reverence. We feel that we are surrounded by the congregated bones of the great men of past times, who have filled history with their deeds, and the earth with their renown. And yet it almost provokes a smile at the vanity of human ambition to see how they are crowded together, and jostled in the dust; what parsimony is observed in doling out a scanty nook — a gloomy corner — a little portion of earth, to those whom, when alive, kingdoms could not satisfy..."
—Washington Irving (1859)
Sketch Book
via Matt Samra

Rev. Michael J. Beasley of the Anglican Diocese of Worcester, England, was attending a liturgy during a retreat at Brookwood, a Russian Orthodox monastery near Surrey. Outside the iconostasis (the partition decorated with icons separating the sanctuary from the rest of the

"Don't worry — we'll be found. My pledge to the church comes due this week."
© 1995 Cartoons by Johns

church), a lay cantor was busy reciting a long passage from the Book of Psalms.

The cantor came across the word "adversaries" and pronounced it "adVERSaries."

" 'ADversaries, my boy," interrupted the priest, Archimandrite Alexis, from somewhere out of sight behind the iconostasis.

"Ad...Ad...AdVERSaries," the cantor struggled unsuccessfully to get the correct pronunciation.

"ADversaries," repeated the priest insistently.

"Ad...Ad...AdVERSaries," stuttered the cantor, getting increasingly flustered.

This went on for several minutes, until a heavy sigh came from behind the iconostasis. "Oh, never mind. You've probably frightened everyone away by now, anyhow," said Archimandrite Alexis, known for his dry sense of humor.

> —via Pastor Clair Hochstetler
> Skyridge Church of the
> Brethren
> Kalamazoo, MI

The ship was sinking fast. The captain called out, "Anyone here know how to pray?"

One man stepped forward: "I do, captain."

"Good," said the captain. "You pray. The rest of us will put on life preservers. We're one short."

> —Archbishop John L. May
> of St. Louis

OUT OF THE MOUTHS OF BABES

In Sunday school, a teacher asked a small girl why she thought the clergyman in the Good Samaritan story passed by on the other side. "Because the man lying by the roadside had already been robbed," the little girl replied.

Humorist Charles Laine, of Franklin, TN, tells this story: Doris Laine (Charles' wife) invited some people to dinner. At the table, she turned to her six-year-old daughter and said, "Would you like to say the blessing?"

"I wouldn't know what to say," the little girl replied.

"Just say what you hear Mommy say," the mother said.

The little girl bowed her head and said: "Dear Lord, why on earth did I invite all these people to dinner?"

Some school children were discussing their parents' jobs in class. One new youngster announced that he was the son of a preacher.

"What abomination do you belong to?" another youngster asked.

—via Rev. Edward A. Black, Jr.
Elysburg (PA) Presbyterian
Church

The boy listened closely as the rabbi read the Bible. "May I ask a question?" he asked.

"Sure. Go ahead. Ask your question," replied the rabbi.

"Well, the Bible says that the children of Israel crossed the Red Sea — the children of Israel built the temple — the children of Israel did this and the children of Israel did that. Didn't the grownups ever do anything?"

A Sunday school teacher was telling her kindergarten children about the Golden Rule. "Remember," she said, "we are here to help others."

"Then what are the others here for?" a little girl asked.

—Msgr. Arthur Tonne
Jokes Priests Can Tell

BULLETIN BLOOPERS THAT GNASH THE TEETH

The newsletter of Anchor Park United Methodist Church in Anchorage, AK, thanked a number of parishioners for their efforts on behalf of the church, including Jo Michalski,

owner of a quilt shop, "for sharing her guilts and their stories with the congregation."
—via Rev. Edmund B. Stanton
Junction City, OR

From the newsletter of Joy Lutheran Church, Richmond, TX: "Bishop Chilstrom will meet with clergy and laity. This unique and gifted pastor...has counseled with numerous Herds of State and Religious Leaders of Christian and nonchristian faiths."
—via Pastor Elwood K. Hall

"Each year, at a meeting of the Presbytery of Greater Atlanta, we remember in prayer our recently deceased elders," reports Rev. Woody McKay of Midway Presbyterian Church in Decatur, GA. "Prior to the meeting, the newsletter of the Presbytery carried the following announcement:
'Only a small number of deceased elders has been sent to us. You can still bring yours with you to the meeting to be added to the list.' "

Pastor Ervin G. Roorda of the Third Reformed Church of Holland, MI, found in several church bulletins these answers that children had provided during Sunday school classes:
"Noah's wife was called Joan of Ark."
"Lot's wife was a pillar of salt by day, and a ball of fire at night."
"Holy acrimony is another name for marriage."

A PRAYER FOR TEACHERS

"God grant you a towering wisdom, to impart all blessings of education.
"And when your wisdom fails like a $1.79 transistor radio —
"God grant you an awesome understanding, to accept the young scoundrel who tests your eminent intellect.
"And when your understanding is tricked and sidetracked into babbling bewilderment —
"God grant you the serenity of divine grace to forbear.

*"And when your grace is threadbare and an alter-ego imp
whispers the delicious promptings of retaliation —*
"God grant you a magnificent strength to endure.
*"And when that last ounce of strength drains pitifully away,
and it is scarcely 2:00 p.m. on the opening day of school —*
*"God grant you the blessed breezes of good humor, to bring the
whole, hopeless mess into a new and delightful perspective!
Amen."*

—Pastor John J. Walker
Post, TX

When Los Angeles was battling Montreal in the National
League championship series in 1981, Dodgers manager Tom
Lasorda gave the following pep talk to his team before the
fifth game:

"Guys, I know we're coming to the end," he
began quietly. "Montreal seems to be in a better
position to win this game and go on to the World
Series. I'm proud of all of you. I'm proud of the
way we've fought to get this far. I will simply quote
from the Holy Bible, from Romans: 'From
tribulation comes strength, and from the depths of
strength comes character...and from the depths of
character comes hope.' Then Lasorda raised his
voice to a shout: "And I hope all of you jackasses
realize that if we don't win this game, we go
home!"
The Dodgers won.

—Joe Garagiola
from *It's Anybody's Ballgame*

ONE-LINERS

"The Lord loveth a cheerful giver. He also accepteth from
the grouch."

—via Catherine Hall
Pittsburgh, PA

"So that's what tithing was all about."
© 1995 Ed Sullivan

"It's church budget season — time for the Sermon on the Amount."
—Rev. Denny J. Brake
Wake Forest, NC

"A lot of people are willing to give God credit, but so few ever give him cash."
—Rev. Robert E. Harris
Laugh with the Circuit Rider
Asheville, NC

"If it is any consolation to clergy today, there is a long history of reluctance to pay tithes — dating at least as far back as the prophet Malachi's time."
—David Briggs
AP Religion Editor

"Don't give until it hurts. Give until it feels good."
—Rev. James Kidd
Asylum Hill Congregational Church
Hartford, CT

"Ask and you will receive, and your joy will be
complete."
—John 16:24

A Prayer For Anointment With The Oil Of Gladness
*"If you are to grow in good temper, you must grow in
good humor. God has given us the power of laughter not
only to laugh at things, but to laugh off things... The art
of laughing at yourself is the highest kind of laughter.
Good humor will make you good-tempered.*

*"O Jesus, Thou wast 'anointed with the oil of gladness
above Thy fellows.' Teach me Thy secret of holy
laughter."*

—E. Stanley Jones
Growing Spiritually
via Pastor Ken Kubichek,
Diamond, OH

~ Chapter 10 ~
October

The devil can't stand
the sound of laughter

B.C.   **By Johnny Hart**

In C.S. Lewis' *The Screwtape Letters*, Screwtape, one of the devil's agents, wrote to one of his lesser demonic pupils as follows:

"I divide the causes of human laughter into Joy, Fun, the Joke Proper, and Flippancy. You will see the first among friends and lovers reunited on the eve of a holiday.

"Among adults some pretext in the way of jokes is usually provided, but the facility with which the smallest witticisms produce laughter at such a time shows that they are not the real cause. What that real cause is we do not know.

"Something like it is expressed in much of that detestable art which the humans call Music, and something like it occurs in Heaven — a meaningless acceleration in the rhythm of celestial experience, quite opaque to us.

"Laughter of this kind does us no good and should always be discouraged. Besides, the phenomenon is of itself disgusting and a direct insult to the realism, dignity, and austerity of Hell."

In 1991, FMC member Connie Soth, a Lutheran librarian in Beaverton, OR, and a columnist for the Church & Synagogue Libraries Association newsletter, proposed to FMC that it help "rescue Halloween from its increasingly ugly and violent tone." She suggested that clowns, comedians, and humorists be brought into Halloween festivities.

Taking up her suggestion, the Fellowship of Merry Christians and its sister organization, the clowns of Smiles Unlimited, combined forces to bring some holy humor into Halloween and give youngsters some alternatives to the usual parade of monsters, vampires, devils, witches, and goblins.

From a list of about 9,000 clowns nationwide, Smiles Unlimited provided to churches, upon request, the names and addresses of clowns in a church's city or area. Protestant and Catholic churches increasingly are sponsoring parties for children on Halloween night. (Churches wishing to use clowns in alternative Halloween activities may write to Don "Ski" Berkoski, President, Smiles Unlimited Clown Ministry,

4149 Golden Eagle Dr., Indianapolis, IN 46234. Please include a stamped and addressed return envelope.)

In the Azores Islands, Portuguese children still observe a different kind of Halloween ("hallowed evening"), the eve of All Saints Day (Nov. 1). They take to the streets and visit neighbors' homes, asking for *pao por Deus* (bread by God). People give out bread as if it were alms to the poor in memory of the faithful departed. Halloween is not just a children's pastime, but also an occasion to practice charity.

"You can cut open a pumpkin and put a candle in it to shed some light, and people will smile. But heaven forbid if they will smile at a stranger. Isn't it time for more people to open up, be more friendly to strangers, and be a light to the world? Wouldn't it be nice to see pumpkin-sized smiles on human beings?"

—Craig E. Galik
Duquesne, PA
Our Sunday Visitor

An FMC member saw this sign outside a church in the Midwest:

DO YOU KNOW WHAT HELL IS LIKE? COME IN AND HEAR OUR CHOIR.

© 1995 Harley L. Schwadron

The gate between heaven and hell broke down. St. Peter appeared at the broken part and called out to the devil, "Hey, Satan. It's your turn to fix it this time."

"Sorry," replied the devil, "my people are too busy to go about fixing a mere gate."

"Well, then," said St. Peter, "I'll have to sue for breaking our agreement."

"Oh yeah," said the devil, "where are you going to get a lawyer?"

—Msgr. Arthur Tonne
Jokes Priests Can Tell

"Once they get through this lawsuit
phase, maybe they'll go back to
loving their neighbor."
© 1994 Harley L. Schwadron

Over the great front doors of an old church being restored was inscribed in stone: "This is the Gate of Heaven." Just below it, someone had placed a small cardboard sign which read: "Use Other Entrance."

A 19th-century African-American preacher was once asked to explain the doctrine of election. He said: "Well, brethren, it is this way: The Lord He is always voting for a man, and the devil he is always voting against him; then the man himself votes, and that breaks the tie."

—Msgr. Arthur Tonne
Joke Priests Can Tell

Rev. Laurence Larson of Rock Island, IL, says this actually happened at a worship service he attended at an Episcopal church:

The priest was wearing a floor-length alb, and during the processional, as he stepped up to the altar, first his left foot and then his right foot stepped on the hem of the robe. He bent over, struggling vainly to disentangle himself, but couldn't move. Finally, two ushers came to the rescue, lifted him up, and carried him to the altar.

"The devil is most happy when he can snatch from a servant of God true joy of the spirit. He carries dust with him to throw into the smallest chinks of conscience and thus soil one's mental candor and purity of life. But if joy of the spirit fills the heart, the serpent shoots his deadly venom in vain."

—St. Francis of Assisi
Second Life, Celano

"I saw the Lord scorn the devil's malice and reduce his powerlessness to nothing, and He wills that we do the same thing. On account of this sight, I laughed loud and long, which made those who were around me laugh, too, and their laughter was a pleasure to me. Then I thought I would like all my fellow Christians to have seen what I saw, for then they should all laugh with me. For I understood that we may laugh, comforting ourselves and rejoicing in God that the devil has been overcome."

—Dame Julian of Norwich 14th-century English mystic

"Year after year they came, descending on me like great hordes of locusts, until I couldn't take it any longer and I had to escape. I can still hear their voices — 'trick or treat, trick or treat.' "

© 1994 Ed Sullivan

Fr. William A. Stickle, Catholic chaplain at the VA Medical Center in Richmond, VA, unearthed and sent the following quotation by Martin Luther, found in *Luther's Works, Vol. 54, Table Talk:*

"God is not a God of sadness, death, etc., but the devil is. Christ is a God of joy, and so the Scriptures often say that we should rejoice...A Christian should and must be a cheerful person."

"Sour godliness is the Devil's religion."
—John Wesley

"It is characteristic of God and His angels that in their activity they give true joy and spiritual exultation, while removing the sadness and affliction that the enemy excites."
—Ignatius of Loyola
Spiritual Exercises
"Rules for the Discernment of Spirits"

"The devil is a thief. He's out to steal your joy. Don't let him. The joy of the Lord is what keeps us young."
—Pastor Steve Feldman
Assembly of God
Jefferson City, MO

"It bothers me that so many people who claim to be Christians look like the devil."
—George Goldtrap

Mary Jean Callahan of Batesville, MS, found one Sunday morning this order of worship in the bulletin of a small Presbyterian church:
Prayer
Sermon: "Hell"
Hymn: "Have Thine Own Way, Lord."

"Living with a saint is more grueling than being one. On the other hand, the definition of a martyr is one who lives with a saint."
—via Msgr. Charles Dollen
Poway, CA

In the early 1800's the people of Reading, England, were deeply disturbed when suddenly there began appearing "strange signs and omens" on their loaves of bread. Some loaves had imprinted on their bottom a picture of the skull and crossbones; others said, "Rest in Peace" or "Died on Christmas Day."

The townspeople feared it was some terrible divine warning of impending judgment. The local constable decided to have a talk with the baker At last the old man confessed. The baker had needed new stones for the floor of his huge oven, but couldn't afford to buy any, so he had stolen the largest, flattest ones he could find from the local graveyard.
—via Paul Thigpen
Springfield, MO

"In a museum in Havana, there are two skulls of Christopher Columbus — one when he was a boy and one when he was a man."
—Mark Twain

Dr. Halford Luccock, Professor of Preaching at Yale Divinity School for over 25 years, was renowned for his sense of humor. He liked to tell the story of a distressed pastor who rushed to his church after a report that it had caught fire. The pastor was surprised to see so many non-church people among the huge crowd gathered to watch his church go up in flames.

The pastor couldn't resist asking one of the onlookers. "Sir, I don't remember seeing you at this church before."

The spectator replied: "Well, this is the first time this church has ever been on fire!"
—via Rev. David J. Droog
Austin, MN

THE FAMILY CIRCUS

"Amazing grace!...How sweet the
sound!...That saved a witch like me..."

Reprinted with permission of Bil Keane

A distraught man went to a psychiatrist and exclaimed, "Doctor, I believe that I am possessed by an evil spirit." After talking to the patient at some length, the psychiatrist said, "You do appear to have a problem. I'd like to see you again next Wednesday."

After the second session of psychotherapy, the psychiatrist pronounced his patient completely cured.

For the next nine months, the psychiatrist sent the man a monthly statement for his professional services, but the man wouldn't pay and refused to acknowledge the debt. Finally, the psychiatrist took the man to court and had him repossessed.

—Rev. Charles B. Hastie
Mackinaw City, MI

HEALTH TEST

*Blow Your Breath
On This Black Cat*

If cat turns purple, there is a
harmful chemical in your breath,
and you should see your doctor
immediately. If she remains black,
you are well enough to attend
church on Sunday.

—via Ann Ball
Houston, TX

"An old, retired professor of church history at Yale was on his death bed. Waiting relatives anxiously gathered around him.

"After a time of silence one man quietly said: 'I think he's gone.'

"Another relative, standing at the end of the bed, felt the old man's feet and said, 'No, his feet are still warm. No one ever dies with warm feet.'

"The eyes of the old professor blinked open. He raised his head up from the bed and looked around at his family. 'Joan of Arc did!' he whispered. He gave a little chuckle and died."

—Jeris Bragan
New Covenant

"The devil can be infinitely sardonic and ironic, but he cannot stand humor. Democracy cannot function without humor, any more than can a machine without lubrication.

"It is the sense of humor which saves men living in a democratic state. Thanks to the sense of humor, a breathable and respectable distance can be re-established between neighbors, between husbands and wives, or between the officials and the normal victims of the State.

"Take any democracy. Suppress every kind of humor... and you will have at the end of the operation, if it is carried through energetically, the totalitarian state in its native splendor."

—Dennis de Rougemont
The Devil's Share
via Dr. John Gilmore
Cincinnati, OH

Why do the inclusive persons
want to call God the Father "He/She"
but seem to be perfectly content
with calling the devil a "he"?
—Anonymous
Seattle, WA

"Overheard in the sacristy: 'The congregation's a bit thin this morning,' said the Vicar. 'Did you tell them I was preaching?' 'No, Vicar, I didn't,' replied the churchwarden, 'but you know how things get out.' "
—*The Anglican Digest*

"It was the Lord who put into my mind to sail from here to the Indies. There is no question that the inspiration was from the Holy Spirit, because He comforted me with rays of marvelous illumination from the Holy Scriptures, encouraging me continually to press forward. No one should fear to undertake any task in the name of our Savior, if it is just and if the intention is purely for His holy service."
—Christopher Columbus
Book of Prophecies

FMC member Rev. Joe LoMusio, pastor of Temple Baptist Church in Fullerton, CA, wrote a book called *If I Should Die Before I Live* to help people avoid getting the following epitaph engraved on their tombstones:
"HERE LIES _____
"DIED AT 35, BURIED AT 68."
"So many Christians," LoMusio says, "are cold and lifeless. They adopt this attitude when they picture God as stern and distant. The stern view of God has become so ingrained in many congregations that a Christian who is alive to God's Spirit, enjoying God and having fun in the faith, is generally treated as unscripturally emotional.
"Why is it that those who continually demonstrate joy are the ones who must defend their position? The excuses ought to come from the joyless and lifeless."

"I cannot help believing that Artemus Ward, Abraham Lincoln's favorite humorist, was reflecting the mind of Christ when he told the Pharisees of his day: 'Your religion is small pertaters, I must say. You air in a dreary fog all the time, and you treat the jolly sunshine of life as though it were a thief, drivin' it from your doors by them pecooler noshuns of yourn.' To which might be added a relative word from Billy Sunday: 'To see some people you would think that the essentials of orthodox Christianity is to have a face so long you could eat oatmeal out of the end of a gas pipe.' "

—Sherwood Elliot Wirt
Jesus — Man of Joy

The wife of an old preacher in Kansas was afraid to fly, but finally summoned the courage to take a flight to Florida to visit her daughter. At the airport, she handed her husband a letter. On the envelope she had written, "Open only in case of a crash."

Teenagers at the feeding of the 5000.
© 1995 Dik LaPine

When he returned home, the old preacher couldn't resist the temptation and opened the letter. The letter said: "If there is a crash, look under our bed. You'll find a box. Open the box."

He looked under the bed, opened the box, and found three eggs and a large stack of $100 bills.

He was mystified. When his wife returned intact from Florida, the old preacher confessed that curiosity had gotten the best of him and he had opened both the envelope and the box. "But, honey, I don't understand," he said. "Why the three eggs and the $100 bills?"

"Well, honey," she replied. "When you first started preaching, every time you laid an egg and preached a poor sermon, I'd put an egg in the box."

"All these years I've preached and I got only three eggs!" he said. "That's not too bad. But I still don't understand the stack of $100 bills."

"When you get a dozen, you gotta sell," she said.

—via Rev. Warren Keating
First Presbyterian Church
Derby, KS

FMC member Rev. Ronald H. Weinelt, a Lutheran pastor in McDonough, GA, and founder of the Association of Battered Clergy, passed on this story:

"On his very first day in office, a new pastor got a call from his predecessor in office. He congratulated him on his new charge and told him that in the center drawer of his desk he had left three envelopes, all numbered, which he was to open in order when he got into trouble.

"After a short-lived honeymoon with the congregation, the heat began to rise and the minister decided to open the first envelope. His predecessor advised him: 'Blame me for the problem. After all, I'm long gone and have problems of my own, and if it will help, point out my shortcomings as the reason things are bad.'

"That worked for awhile, but then things got sour again. The pastor opened the second envelope, which read: 'Blame the denomination. They're big and rich. They can take it.'

"That worked well for awhile, but then the storm clouds gathered again, and in desperation the pastor went to the drawer and opened the third envelope. It said: 'Prepare three envelopes!' "

"After God created the world, He made man and woman. Then, to keep the whole thing from collapsing, He invented humor."
—Mordillo
via Bill Kelly
Deerfield, IL

THE FAMILY CIRCUS

"Do guardian angels take days off?"

IF YOU WISH TO SPEAK WITH GOD, PLEASE PRESS 1

Fr. Dominic Maruca, SJ, a professor at Pontifical Gregorian University in Rome, writes in *The Priest* magazine that one day he was having difficulty with a new computer and called the 800 number provided by the manufacturer.

While waiting for a human voice to come on the line, Fr. Maruca began to daydream: "What would it be like if terrestrial hi-tech finally reached the heavenly realms, for example, when I tried to pray?"

In his daydream, Fr. Maruca said he heard this recording:

"Thank you for calling technical support. We are available to assist you every day of the week except, of course, on the Sabbath. If you have a Touch Tone telephone, you can reach your desired party by pressing the proper number.

"If you wish to speak with God the Father, please press 1.

"If you wish to speak with Jesus, His Son, please press 2.

"If you wish to speak with His Holy Spirit, please press 3.

"If you wish to speak with Mary, the mother of Jesus, please press 4.

"If you wish to speak with one of the saints, please press 5.

"If you have some question about the Ten Commandments, press 6.

"If you have some complaint about the liturgical changes, please press 7.

"If your trouble is with the Church Universal, press 8.

"If you are having difficulty with your local bishop or pastor, press 9."

Fr. Maruca said he awakened from his daydream somewhat shaken. After shutting down his printer and computer, he went down to the chapel. As he knelt there, he thought he heard a chuckle coming from the direction of the tabernacle. It was probably just his overactive imagination.

Anyway, he caught himself smiling and heard himself saying, *"Thanks, Lord, for always being so readily accessible. Please don't go hi-tech on us — ever."*

Rev. Vincent Heier, of the Catholic Archdiocese of St. Louis, recently welcomed a group of visiting Missouri-

Kansas Lutherans meeting in St. Louis Cathedral with these words:
>"We are pleased to provide the cathedral. Please don't nail anything to the doors."

WHY GOD NEVER RECEIVED TENURE AT A UNIVERSITY

JN consulting editors Steve Feldman of Jefferson City, MO, and George and Peggy Goldtrap of Madison, TN, put their heads together and came up with "Seventeen Reasons Why God Never Received Tenure at a University."

1) He published only one book.
2) Some scholars seriously doubt that He wrote it Himself.
3) It was first published in Hebrew, then in Greek, and then revised and rewritten endlessly by translators.
4) It carried no references and was never published in an authorized journal.
5) He was vague about His background and credentials and kept repeating, "I am that I am."
6) He was accused repeatedly of being a Male Chauvinist.
7) He would not submit to psychological examinations or psychotherapy conducted by one of His peers.
8) He did not keep regular office hours and sometimes insisted on holding His classes on mountaintops.
9) He wanted 10 percent of the university's income as His salary.
10) He never got permission from the National Institutes of Health to experiment with human subjects.
11) He put His first student to sleep.
12) He expelled His first two students.
13) He insisted on 10 rules for maintaining campus discipline.
14) He gave final exams on the honor system.
15) He refused to grade on a curve.
16) He sent His Son to teach the class.
17) Scientists cannot replicate His results.

"You shall laugh at drought and frost."
—Job 5:22

A PRAYER FOR BACKBONE

Baptist Pastor Tal Bonham reported that "an elderly country preacher" prayed the following prayer every day. Another pastor later identified the "elderly country preacher" as "the long-time Nazarene evangelist Uncle Bud Robinson, a stammering, uneducated Texas cowboy who brought thousands of people to God in the early part of this century."

"O Lord, give me a backbone as big as a saw log and ribs like the large timbers under the church floor. Put iron shoes on my feet and galvanized breeches on my body. Give me a rhinoceros hide for skin, and hang up a wagon load of determination in the gable-end of my soul. Help me to sign the contract to fight the devil as long as I've got a tooth — and then gum him until I die."

~ Chapter 11 ~
November

Thanksgiving, football, God-fearing and God-sneering politicians

THE FAMILY CIRCUS

Reprinted with permission of Bil Keane (*Behold the Family Circus*)

There is an old European story about a traveler who came upon a barn where the devil had stored seeds which he planned to sow in the hearts of people. There were bags of seeds variously marked "Hatred," "Fear," "Doubt," "Despair," "Unforgiveness," "Pride," "Greed," etc.

The devil appeared and struck up a conversation with the traveler. He gleefully told the traveler how easily the seeds he sowed sprouted in the hearts of men and women.

"Are there any hearts in which these seeds will not sprout?" the traveler asked.

A melancholy look appeared on the devil's face. "These seeds will not sprout in the heart of a thankful and joyful person," he confessed.

THANKSGIVING ONE-LINERS

"Just be thankful you're not getting all the government you're paying for."
—Will Rogers

"I remember an elderly lady testifying that she had only two teeth left in her mouth (top and bottom), and she was 'rejoicing' because 'they hit.' "
—Sherwood Eliot Wirt

"You never know how much you have to be thankful for until you pay taxes on it."
—Rev. Denny J. Brake
Raleigh, NC

"The worship most acceptable to God comes from a thankful and cheerful heart."
—Plutarch (46-120 A.D.)

"The most important prayer in the world is just two words long: 'Thank you.' "
—Meister Eckhart (1327 A.D.)

"Joy is really the simplest form of gratitude."
—Karl Barth

© 1995 Harley L. Schwadron

"The first Thanksgiving was held in 1621. The Pilgrims gave thanks for having survived another year, and the Indians gave thanks for having survived another Pilgrim."
—James R. Swanson
Costa Mesa, CA

"To stand on one's legs and prove God's existence is a very different thing from going on one's knees and thanking Him."
—Soren Kierkegaard

"Gratitude is a vaccine, an antitoxin, and an antiseptic."
—John Henry Jowett

"It's important for your health to have an attitude of gratitude. When you get up in the morning, do you say, 'Good Lord, morning!'? Or do you say, 'Good morning, Lord!'?"
—George Goldtrap

A very devout Christian woman went to a pet store. She saw a parrot which she adored and decided to buy. The owner said, "Lady, I couldn't sell you that parrot. He was owned by a sailor and he cusses a blue streak."

But the woman could not be dissuaded. She believed that the parrot, with Christian love and firm discipline, could be retrained. She took the parrot home.

The parrot began cussing and swearing. She warned the parrot that she was going to put him in the freezer for 10 minutes to teach him to hold his tongue.

When the parrot continued to swear, the woman put the caged parrot in the freezer. After 10 minutes, she took him out.

The shivering parrot seemed remorseful. "Pppplease, llllady," the parrot said. "Wwwwould yyyyou ttttell

mmmme jjjjust oooone tttthing? Wwwwhat ddddid tttthe
tttturkey ddddo?"

—via Rick Beemer,
Managing Editor
Our Sunday Visitor

"We are always saving somebody away off, when the
fellow next to us ain't eating."

—Will Rogers

Thanksgiving Day was approaching, and the family had
received a Thanksgiving card with a painting of a Pilgrim
family on their way to church.

Grandma showed the card to her small grandchildren,
observing: "The Pilgrim children like to go to church with
their mothers and fathers."

"Oh yeah?" her young grandson replied, "so why is their
dad carrying that rifle?"

"When the kids in my Catholic family used to say grace at
meals — 'Bless us, O Lord, for these Thy gifts which we are
about to receive from Your bounty'— it would sometimes
sound like 'Blorgifarebonty.'

"When the Protestants say the blessings at meals, they can
be said in different ways, but you must thank the Lord for
everything within sight:

" 'Thank you, O Lord, for the people who have gathered
here this evening.'

" 'Thank you for the food and drink we are about to partake.'

" 'Thank you for the silverware.'

" 'Thank you for the silversmith who forged the
silverware.'

" 'Thank you for the mining company that mined the silver…' "

—Tommy DiNardo

Visiting a big city, a Christian farmer entered a fancy
restaurant for lunch. When his meal was served, he bowed
his head and quietly gave thanks to God for the food.

There was a group of rowdy teenagers at a nearby table, and one of them taunted him in a loud voice: "Hey, farmer, does everyone do that where you live?"

The old farmer looked at the young man and calmly said: "No, son, the pigs don't."

—via Dr. John J. Walker
Post, TX

Texas goat rancher and humorist Ron Birk, a semi-retired Lutheran pastor, says he's planning to write a book titled *Real Pastors Will Eat Anything*.

Real pastors, he writes —

★ take at least a bite from every dish at church potluck dinners.

★ will eat anything while attending a convention on an expense account. *"And into whatsoever city ye enter, and they receive you, eat such things as are set before you."* — *Luke 10:8*

★ don't subscribe to a sermon service.

★ always witness to the stranger who sits next to them on airplanes.

★ look forward to hearing the telephone ring.

★ don't have to worry about what goes in the parsonage trash can.

★ have actually read every book in their libraries.

★ always wear their clerical collars when visiting in the hospital and while driving through speed traps.

★ don't use answering machines.

"On Saturday evening, I reserve the privilege of preparing the bread (we use leavened bread) for our Sunday celebration of the Eucharist. I set aside some of the crusts so that my wife can put them to good use in her delicious Caesar salads. Whenever I am asked what I do on Saturday evenings, I simply say, 'I render unto Caesar the things that are Caesar's and unto God the things that are God's.' "

—Rev. William G. Campbell
St. Saviour's Anglican Church
Vermilion, Alberta

In league with Rev. Earl Banning, Bill Ellis, state coordinator for the Church of God (Anderson) in West Virginia, composed some "football-speak theology" for *Religious Broadcasting* magazine, including:

Bench warmer: An inactive church member.

Quarterback sneak: Sunday school teachers entering the church building five minutes after Sunday school begins.

Fumble: A lousy sermon.

Two-minute warning: The chairman of the board sitting in a front-row pew, taking a look at his watch in full view of the preacher.

Illegal motion: Leaving before the benediction.

Blocking: Standing inside the church door complaining to the pastor about the sermon.

Extra point: What you receive when you tell the preacher the sermon was too short.

THAT WAS FOOTBALL?

"Things were pretty simple in those days. We went to class and played football, and that was it. None of the guys ever got into trouble. No trash talk or taunting. No girl problems, no drugs, no jail. It just wasn't part of what we did, and even if we wanted to do it, Biggie Munn (the coach) wouldn't allow it."

—Lynn Chandnois
Michigan State All-American
back (1946-49)
The Detroit News

Rev. Ted Jones of First Presbyterian Church, Normal, IL, passed on the following item, written anonymously, which he found in the newsletter of St. Luke's Union Church, Bloomington, IL:

**12 Reasons Why A Local Pastor Stopped
Attending Sports Events**

1. Every time I went, they asked me for money.
2. The people with whom I had to sit didn't seem very friendly.

3. The seats were very hard.
4. The coach never came to call on me.
5. The referee made a decision with which I could not agree.
6. I was sitting with some hypocrites — they came only to see what others were wearing.
7. Some games went into overtime and I was late getting home.
8. The band played some songs I had never heard before.
9. The games are scheduled when I want to do other things.
10. My parents took me to too many games when I was growing up.
11. Since I read a book on sports, I feel that I know more than the coaches, anyhow.
12. I don't want to take my children because I want them to choose for themselves what sport they like best.

POLITICS AND RELIGION

During a heated debate in the U.S. Senate, one senator told another to "go to hell." The senator under attack appealed to the presiding vice president, Calvin Coolidge, concerning the propriety of the remark.

Coolidge, who had been idly leafing through a book, looked up and said, "I've been going through the rule book. You don't have to go."

—Archbishop John L. May of St. Louis

"Pat, you're going to make yourself sick wondering if your guardian angel is a liberal or a conservative."

© 1995 Ed Sullivan

FMC member Evelyn A. Briscoe of Okmulgee, OK, writes that she was on a boat in the middle of the Sea of Galilee in Israel and a Baptist told her this story:

Israeli Prime Minister Yitzhak Shamir and President George Bush scheduled a meeting. Shamir arrived late, and Bush let him know in no uncertain terms that he did not like to be kept waiting.

Shamir replied, "I'm sorry, Mr. President. I was meetng with someone more important than you are."

"Who is more important than the President of the United States?" Bush asked.

Shamir replied: "I was meeting with Moses."

"You know Moses!?" Bush exclaimed. "Get him on the phone. I want to talk to him."

Shamir picked up the phone, dialed, listened, and then hung up. "He doesn't want to talk to you," he told Bush. "He said the last time he talked to a bush it cost him 40 years in the wilderness."

A Sunday school teacher asked her class: "Who decreed that all the world should be taxed?"

"The Democrats," a young girl answered.

"If God had wanted us to vote, He would have given us candidates."

—Jay Leno

Three friends — a surgeon, an engineer, and a politician — were discussing which of their professions was the oldest.

The surgeon said: "Eve was created from Adam's rib — a surgical procedure."

The engineer replied: "Before Adam and Eve were created, order was created out of chaos, and that was an engineering job."

The politician said: "Yes, but who do you suppose created the chaos?"

—via Catherine Hall
Pittsburgh, PA

A preacher woke up one Monday morning and told his wife that he had dreamt this dream:

Three presidential candidates died and went to heaven. They were brought before the Lord, who was seated on His throne.

"Who are you and what did you do to deserve to be here?" the Lord asked the first presidential candidate.

"I'm George Bush and I'm the former President of the United States," he replied, and then proceeded to relate all the things he had done for his country and the world.

"Welcome," the Lord said. "Take the seat on my right." He then asked the second presidential candidate: "And who are you?"

"I'm Bill Clinton and I'm the current President of the United States," he replied, and proceeded to relate all the things he was doing for his country and the world.

"Welcome," the Lord said. "Take the seat on my left." Then, turning to the third man, the Lord asked: "Who are you?"

"I'm Ross Perot and I believe you're sitting in my seat."

—via George Goldtrap

When Bill Moyers was a special assistant to President Lyndon B. Johnson, he was asked to say grace at a dinner in the White House. Moyers began praying softly. Johnson interrupted him: "Speak up, Bill! Speak up!"

Moyers, a former minister from east Texas, stopped in mid-sentence and without looking up replied, "I wasn't addressing you, Mr. President."

—Anglican Digest

During a political debate, one heckler's nonstop verbal abuse was irking candidates and audience alike. The loudmouth met his match, however, when he interrupted a speaker with a raucous "I wouldn't vote for you if you were St. Peter!"

"If I were St. Peter," the candidate shot back, "You wouldn't be in my district."

—Liguorian

© 1995 Ed Sullivan

Campaigning through his state, the late Sen. Clyde Hoey of North Carolina stopped at a church in a small town and was greeted by the minister. "How many members do you have in your church?" the senator asked.

"Fifty," the pastor replied.

"And how many active members?"

"Fifty."

"Fifty members and fifty active? You must be a good preacher!" the senator said.

"Yes, sir — fifty members," the minister said. "Twenty-five active for me and twenty-five active against me."

—William C.S. Pellowe
Laughter under the Steeple

If the U.S. Government were in place when God talked to Moses, the conversation would have gone something like this: God said: "Moses, I have some good news and some bad news for you. The good news is that you are going to lead my people Israel out of Egypt, and you are going to have to part the Red Sea to do it."

"And the bad news?" Moses asked.

"You will have to fill out all of the environmental impact forms before leaving."

—via Donald L. Cooper, M.D.
Stillwater, OK

John Dart, religion writer for *The Los Angeles Times*, reports that he went to a comedy night at Bel Air Presbyterian Church in Encino, CA, where Ronald and Nancy Reagan were once regular worshipers. "An audience of 900 adults in

the pews roared with laughter" during the acts of several
Clean Comedians, Dart reported.

Stand-up comedian Robert G. Lee imagined Moses in
heaven still grumbling: "We wandered the desert for 40
years. Every day, a million people would come up to me and
say, 'Are we there yet?' "

Lee tells audiences that Bel Air Presbyterian built an oval
pew for the ex-President and put jelly beans by his hymnal.
But, he said, when the Secret Service installed metal
detectors at the sanctuary entrance, long, amusement-park
lines appeared outside the church. Lee said, "There was a
sign at the end: 'You are now 45 minutes from the sermon.' "

POLITICAL PRAYERS

Recent opening prayers by legislators in the Michigan
Legislature:

Rep. William Keith, Garden City Democrat: "Dear Lord, as
we go about Your business in taking care of the people of the
State of Michigan, please put Your right hand on our
shoulder and Your left hand over our mouth. Amen."

Rep. Maxine Berman, Southfield Democrat: "Lord, please
bless this House and do what You can with the Senate."

Rep. James Agee, Muskegon Democrat: "Lord, we ask that
You give us wisdom and strength so that we may bring
today's session to a fruitful and speedy conclusion."
—*Kalamazoo Gazette*

An old prayer for politicians: "Teach us, O Lord, to utter
words that are tender and gentle, for tomorrow we may
have to eat them."

WILL ROGERS ON PREACHERS AND POLITICIANS

The late humorist Grady Nutt, a Baptist pastor, said of
Will Rogers: "He (Jesus) makes the most sense to me, the
most profound impact on me, when I envision Him as Will
Rogers in sandals."

Will Rogers, who helped Americans laugh through the
Great Depression of the 1930's, was one of the most loved

people in our nation's history — a gentle, fun-loving man whose wit poured from a loving and joyful heart.

JN consulting editor Cy Eberhart, a United Church of Christ chaplain in Salem, OR, researched Rogers' life at the Will Rogers Memorial in Claremore, OK, and now offers a portrayal of Rogers to churches and organizations. "Rogers had little interest in theological niceties," says Eberhart, "but his views of the religious life were rooted in personal experiences and expressed the pragmatism and tolerance of a widely traveled man."

Another *JN* consulting editor, Edward R. Walsh of Westbury, NY, also has done extensive research on Rogers' life. Says Walsh: "Will Rogers never met a pastor he didn't like. He sorta was on their side, you see. He rubbed shoulders with them just as he did with the politicians. And like he had for the politicos, he had a few choice words about preachers every now and then."

Here are some of Will Rogers' observations on religion, preachers, and politicians collected by Eberhart, Walsh, and *JN* editor Cal Samra.

In a newspaper column of Oct. 2, 1932, Rogers lamented: "After finishing listening to the World Series (on the radio), I figure on account of it being Sunday I could leave it turned on and not have to listen to some politician. But what do I get? Four preachers, all at different places. What was they doing? Saving the sinner? No. Two of 'em was saving the Republicans and the other two was saving the Democrats. The old sinner won't get much consideration till after Nov. 4."

Asked about the foreign missionary work of his day, Rogers commented: "Why, we can't even Christianize our legislators."

"When Congress gets the Constitution all fixed up, they are going to start on the Ten Commandments, just as soon as they can find someone in Washington who has read them."

"Moses just went up on the mountain with a letter of credit and some instructions from the Lord, and he wrote 'em out... He made 'em short. They may not always be kept, but they are understood. They are the same for all. In Moses' time, the rich didn't gang up on you and say, 'you change that commandment or we won't play.' "

"I don't believe that Noah took a pair of every kind of animal into the Ark. I don't believe Noah could round up all the animals in one herd without the skunk causing a stampede."

"I come not to destroy the law but to fulfill it."

© 1991 Goddard Sherman

"Political conventions remind us that the White House is a little like heaven — not everybody who talks about it is going there."

"Church people all over the country are divided and arguing over where we come from. Never mind where we come from, neighbor. Women living next door to you will find out where you come from, and all about you, better than (William Jennings) Bryan and all the preachers. Just let the preachers make it their business where you are going when you leave."

"Americans don't fear the Lord as much as they do the next payment."

"I heard a fellow preach one time on Jesse James, the outlaw, and I left the church wanting to hold up everything and everybody I ran into."

"Congressmen and fellows like me are alike in some ways, I guess. But when I make a joke, it's a joke. When they make a joke, it's a law."

"Our Savior had a plan. He wanted to help us. He said, 'Love thy neighbor as thyself.' But I'll bet there ain't two people on your block that are speaking to each other."

"The Fourth Reader — *McGuffey's* — is as far as I ever got in school. I was raised predominantly a Methodist, but I have traveled so much, mixed with so many people in all parts of the world, I don't know just what I am. I know I have never been a non-believer.

"If I am broad-minded in any way, I do know that I am broad-minded in a religious way. Which way you serve your God will never get one argument, or condemnation, out of me. There has been times when I wished there had been as much religion among some of our creeds as there has been vanity."

Talking about the tendency of Christian denominations to divide and multiply, Rogers observed: "So things don't change much after all. Things just get different names, but remain about the same.

"But if the two sets of churches or a half-dozen sets of churches went together and worshiped, why, one set of preachers would be done away with, or maybe five sets of them would have to hunt for other vocations, for the more you combine the less help you need. The Civil War has been over 63 years, but the churches are the only ones that haven't found it out."

"The happiest Methodists in Tulsa" (so says the church's slogan) go to Will Rogers United Methodist Church.

Yes, there is a Will Rogers United Methodist Church, named after the great American humorist. And FMC member Larry Jacobson, also a humorist, is the pastor.

The church recently celebrated its jubilee (50th) year.

"If it please the court, my client would like to withdraw that last remark about letting him who is without sin cast the first stone."

© 1990 Ed Sullivan (*A Gift of Laughter*)

As might be expected, Will Rogers church members have a lot of fun. "We do laugh a lot," says Rev. Jacobson.

Commenting on Roger's famous remark, "I never met a man I didn't like," associate pastor Terry Ewing suggested the church's slogan ought to be: "We are the folks Will Rogers never met."

Jacobson likes to play satiric little games with his congregation. He recently printed and passed out to the congregation the following list of new books he recommended in the church library:

Perfection and How I Attained It by Rev. L. Jacobson
Join the Crowd: How to Have a Dysfunctional Family
Tithing from Credit Cards
Road to Abundant Life — Jonah's Seaweed Diet
Learn the Bible While You Sleep
Self-Counseling and How to Perform Surgery at Home
Walking by Faith: Climbing Stairs in Bifocals
Building Self-Esteem When You don't Deserve It
Raising Great Kids on Five Minutes a Day
Learn to Teach Sunday School without Preparation

Winning Souls without Getting Involved with People
How to Forgive without Anyone Knowing It
Gossip in the Spirit
Revival by Video in Your Own Home

The Latin inscription "ANNUIT COEPTIS" over the pyramid on the reverse side of the dollar bill, was designed in 1782. Translation: "God has smiled on our undertakings."

> *There is no problem*
> *So gross or perverse*
> *That someone in power*
> *Cannot make worse.*
> —Gene Lehman
> *Luno*, Boring, OR

Pastor Feldman wonders whether to shorten his sermons or ban cordless phones from the worship service.
© 1993 Ed Koehler

Many folks remember the famous Burma-Shave roadside signs with the safety jingles and entertaining rhymes — one of America's most successful and long-running advertising campaigns. But not many people know that the creators of the Burma-Shave signs were fun-loving Christians.

The late Allan G. Odell, who went to the Lord smiling at the age of 90 in 1994, originated the idea for the six-sign sets to sell his brushless shaving cream way back in 1927, and was among the first to use humor in ad campaigns effectively.

Odell's widow, Grace, an FMC member, attends St.
Stephen's Episcopal Church in Edina, MN.
Here are some favorite Burma-Shave signs:

The road was slippery
curve was sharp
white robe, halo,
wings and harp
Burma-Shave

Heaven's latest
neophyte
signaled
left then
turned right
Burma-Shave

In this vale
of toil and sin
your head grows bald
but not
your chin
Burma-Shave

When Allan Odell died, the *Portsmouth Virginia-Pilot*
saluted him with this jingle:

There was nary a hair
on his Burma-Shaved face
when he asked St. Peter
for a key to the place.

The Odells were married 65 years. "We had such a happy,
happy time," said Grace. "I'm still laughing."

A barbershop quartet known as "Four Heaven's Sake!"
specializes in zany religious comedy and is tickling
funnybones in California. Three of them are pastors.
    These merrymakers show up dressed in the outfits of a
televangelist, the Pope's chef, a monk, and a rabbi.

FMC member Dick Friedline, minister of Westchester (CA) Christian Church, comes on in a tuxedo in his role as a televangelist. "If everyone in this audience would just send $250, we could all vacation in Hawaii," he exhorts the audience.

Paul Coleman, the baritone, makes his entrance as "Guiseppi Zucchini," cook and chauffeur for the Pope in Rome. He kisses a bald man in the audience on top of the head and says: "How are you? The Pope sends his best."

Their comedy is madcap, but they sing old-time barbershop and spiritual songs in harmony.

The last rites given a Catholic include a final blessing called the Apostolic blessing, or "the Pope's blessing,"

Father Thomas McBride, a missionary in Bolivia, anointed an old Indian on his sick bed and then added that he would give the man the Pope's blessing. This was duly translated by the Indian interpreter to the old man.

The old man murmured something.

"What did he say?" the priest asked the interpreter.

"He said 'thank you,' but he wants to know how the Holy Father knew he was sick."

—Msgr. Arthur Tonne
Jokes Priests Can Tell

William J. Murray, son of atheist Madalyn Murray O'Hair and author of *My Life without God*, became a Christian "because he couldn't stand the silences after the sneezes," according to Dean Edward Gaffney of the Valparaiso University Law School.

A sign in an apartment window in Los Angeles read: "Drums for sale." In an adjoining apartment window, another sign proclaimed: "Thank God."

Sign in a pastor's office:
"Thank God it's Monday."

"Let us come into His presence with thanksgiving; let us make a joyful noise to Him with songs of praise!"
—Psalm 95:2

THANKSGIVING PRAYER

"Father, bless us according to our thanklessness, lest Thou bless us according to our thankfulness, and we starve."

—Anonymous

~ Chapter 12 ~
December

'It's beginning to look a lot like (bleep)'

THE FAMILY CIRCUS

Reprinted with permission of Bil Keane

"Listen to the angel's song, all you who have a troubled heart! 'I bring you good tidings of great joy!' Jesus did not come to condemn you. If you want to define Christ rightly, then pay heed to how the angel defines Him, namely, 'a great joy!' "
—Martin Luther

"Somehow, not only for Christmas
But all the long year through
The joy that you give to others
Is the joy that comes back to you."
—John Greenleaf Whittier

"Christmas is love in action. Every time we love, every time we give, it's Christmas."
—Dale Evans Rogers

A woman went to the Post Office to buy stamps for her Christmas cards. "What denomination?" asked the clerk.

"Oh, good heavens! Have we come to this?" said the woman. "Well, give me 50 Catholic and 50 Baptist ones."
—via Pastor Jim Patrick
Salt and Light
Indianola, IA

The complete catalog of gifts in the old Christmas carol "The Twelve Days of Christmas" today would cost you a total of $15,231.72.

J. Patrick Bradley, chief economist at Provident National Bank in Philadelphia, figures the breakdown of prices for the 12 days as follows:

* One partridge in a pear tree, $27.48 (Partridge, $15; pear tree, $12.48).
* Two turtle doves, $50.
* Three French hens, $15.
* Four calling birds, $280.

✩ Five gold rings, $600.
✩ Six geese-a-laying, $150.
✩ Seven swans-a-swimming, $7,000.
✩ Eight maids-a-milking, $30.40.
✩ Nine ladies dancing, $2,417.90.
✩ 10 lords-a-leaping, $2,686.56.
✩ 11 pipers piping, $947.70.
✩ 12 drummers drumming, $1,026.68.

"In our town it is the custom to give a Christmas present of a few dollars to the trash collector. Some collectors remind their customers by taping a card to trash cans: 'Seasons Greetings from your trash collector.' Last year I forgot to respond to the first 'greetings' card. Just a day or two before Christmas, there appeared a second card on my trash can: 'Seasons Greetings from your trash collector. SECOND NOTICE.' "

—Cliff Thomas, R.Ph.
Belle Fourche, SD

Quaker humorist Tom Mullen was visiting his brother Frank, who lives in New York. Frank told Tom that New York City has the biggest and longest garbage strikes in the country, and the garbage piles up on the streets.

Frank said that when a garbage strike was called before Christmas one year, he solved the problem by wrapping his garbage daily as if it were a Christmas gift and putting it in the back seat of his car, leaving the car door unlocked. Invariably a thief would steal the package.

MERRY MARY FULL OF JOY

"On that first Christmas morning, Mary must have felt merry indeed. Although Mary is usually pictured as calm and serene on Christmas morning, we might remember that she was at that time a teenager. Two thousand years later, it seems difficult for many of us to imagine the intensity of the joy of a teenager who knows that she has given birth to the Messiah, her joy as she watched Him grow to manhood, her joy at the great healing miracles He performed, her joy at the resurrection, and her joy as she watched belief in Him spread through the nations."

> —Bernadette McCarver Snyder
> *Merry Mary Meditations*

A father and his son were looking at a Nativity scene in a London gallery. It was Titian's world-famous painting of the scene at Bethlehem. The boy asked: "Dad, why is the baby lying in such a cruddy cradle in a pile of straw?"

"Well, son," explained the father, "they were poor and they couldn't afford anything better."

Said the boy: "Then how come they could afford to have their picture painted by such an expensive artist?"

> —Msgr. Arthur Tonne
> *Jokes Priests Can Tell*

"Is not Jesus pointing to children even as models for grownups?"

> —Pope John Paul II

OUT OF THE MOUTHS OF BABES

When a pastor asked the class, "Why was Jesus born in Bethlehem?" a boy raised his hand and replied, "Because his mother was there."

> —Rev. William Armstrong, S.J.

A Sunday school teacher asked her class why Joseph and Mary took Jesus with them to Jerusalem. "They couldn't get a baby-sitter," a small child replied.

> —via Catherine Hall
> Pittsburgh, PA

A Sunday school teacher was telling her class of fourth-graders the Christmas story about the three Wise Men bringing gifts to the Baby Jesus.

A little girl who had recently become the big sister of a brand-new baby brother said: "Well, I guess gold and all that

stuff are all right, but I'll bet Mary really wished somebody had brought some diapers."
—via Jim McDonough
Stone Mountain, GA

"One of the members of our church invited his brother and his family to our Christmas service. During the service, the four-year-old boy began squirming in the pew and whispered to his daddy that he had to go to the potty.

"The father took the boy's hand and escorted him up the aisle to the rest room. About halfway down the aisle, the little guy stopped, turned around, and said loud and clear: 'I have to go potty, God, but I'll be right back!' "
—Mrs. Marjorie Diggins
Marshalltown, IA

A mother discovered her five-year-old daughter drawing with her crayons on some paper. "What are you drawing?" she asked.

"A picture of God," the little girl said.
The mother replied: "No one knows what God looks like."
"They will when I get through," the girl said.
—via Catherine Hall
Pittsburgh, PA

When he was a pastor at Grace Church in Altus, OK, FMC member Rev. Larry Eisenberg asked the children what "Amen" means during a children's sermon.

A little boy raised his hand and said: "It means — 'Tha-tha-tha- that's all, folks!' "

"The further West he went, the more convinced he became that the wise men came from the East."
—Rev. Sydney Smith
19th-century English clergyman

© 1993 Sandy Dean

CHRISTMAS LAUGHTER
> *This is the melody of Christmas!*
> *Wide-eyed, sleighbell laughter*
> > *of tiny ones experiencing the bright surprises;*
> *Whisper-laughter of parents*
> > *exchanging their knowing glances;*
> *Tear-dimmed chuckles*
> > *of reminiscence;*
> *Freshets of family-get-together laughter;*
> *Ties-that-bind laughter*
> > *of the church family;*
> *Joy-in-heaven laughter*
> > *of a great company of angels*
> > *watching the first shepherd-visitors*
> > *making their way to a manger.*
> > > —Dr. John J. Walker
> > > Post, TX

Fr. John Miller recalls that when he was fresh out of seminary and on his first assignment, he was asked to read Bishop Peter Bartholome's letter of blessing to the congregation at a Christmas Day mass at St. John Cantius Church in St. Cloud, MN.

He dutifully began to read the bishop's letter: "I wish to extend to all of you the joys and blessings of the Christmas season..." But when he came to the closing, "Sincerely yours in Christ, Peter W. Bartholome, Bishop of St. Cloud," he read instead, "Sincerely yours in Christ, Peanut Butter Bartholome..."

Peals of laughter came from the pews. "I blew it," says Fr. Miller.

> —via Joseph Young
> Saint Cloud (MN) *Visitor*

When the Bishop of Chester, England, declared that there should be a religious message on Christmas stamps, *Punch* magazine suggested "Lord *deliver* us" as an appropriate message."

The late Cardinal Francis Spellman of New York once accompanied comedian Bob Hope on a Christmas trip to Vietnam, where Hope was to entertain American troops. Hope and his wife, Dolores, who is Catholic, went to a mass celebrated by the cardinal.

Hope fell asleep during the mass. Later, the cardinal told Hope that he had also fallen asleep when he once caught the comedian's act in a New York theater.

IN DEFENSE OF SANTA CLAUS

"It's not Santa Claus' fault that people forget the Infant Jesus. Why does the world love Santa Claus?

"First of all, he's a joyous individual. People are attracted to joyous individuals as filings are attracted to a magnet. Next, Santa Claus is interested in making others happy. He increases the happy moments in the life of everyone he meets. He loves his work; he gets fun out of his job.

"He is childlike, simple, humble, sincere, and forgiving. Finally, he is a giver. His philosophy is to give himself away in service. He is a friend to everyone. He smiles.

"Perhaps you and I could attain greater happiness if we emulated Santa Claus a little more, for his way is the way of the Infant Jesus also."

—Msgr. Joseph P. Dooley
Martins Creek, PA

There are three periods in a person's life:
1) When you believe in Santa Claus.
2) When you don't believe in Santa Claus.
3) When you *are* Santa Claus.
—Rev. James A. Simpson

A Sunday school teacher asked a little boy: "Bobby, do you believe in the devil?"

"No," the boy said. "He's just like Santa Claus. I think it's my Daddy."

Appearing in television's *The Original Tonight Show*, comedian Steve Allen recreated an old Christmas act with Bill Dana. Interviewing Dana's character, "José" Allen learns that José is an instructor at "The New York School for Santa Clauses," then asks what José teaches the Santa Clauses.

"I teach them how to say…" José explains, and then raises a sign with the words "JO! JO! JO!"

FMC member Rev. George E. Franke, director of pastoral care at Victory Memorial Hospital, Waukegan, IL, wrote *JN*:

"People who have had to struggle with the restricted choices imposed by the new health care plans will understand the story circulating around our hospital that the reason Jesus had to be born in a manger was because Mary and Joseph were part of an HMO (Health Maintenance Organization)."

To discourage mall shoppers from parking in the nearby lot of the Church of the Good Shepherd, a formidable sign was posted, reading: "Parking reserved for Good Shepherd only."
—Fr. John Hampsch, CMF
Claretian Tape Ministry
Los Angeles, CA

"Purchasing Christmas gifts for clergy is an extremely difficult task," observes *JN* consulting editor Rev. David R. Francoeur, an Episcopal priest with a gift of satire in Gainesville, FL. So, annually in *JN's* Christmas issue, Rev. Francoeur offers some special Christmas gift suggestions for clergy from the catalog of Balmy Clergy Supply, Inc. Here are some of the ads:

CHRISTMAS GIFTS FOR CLERGY FROM BALMY CLERGY SUPPLY

PRAYING PANTS
Research indicates that clergy are the swiftest of all Christians to get down on their knees and pray for the needs of

others. As a result, they wear out their pants faster than others. Pants are costly. Therefore Balmy has designed The Praying Pants for durability. The Praying Pants are made of woven Kevlar fiber with air bags on the knees that inflate prior to impact. A sensor detects the change in the angle of the knee, and a soft cushion of air gently lowers the pastor to a praying position.

XZPP-58 $75.33

NECKBAND COLLAR MONEY SAFES

These easy-to-wear neckband collars double as a convenient storage place for folded cash. Thieves may strip you bare and never find your money! Available in all sizes. Intrusion alarm optional.

21V   Box of 3 $25.67
21V-A (with alarm)   Box of 3
$92.10

EARLY EXIT ALARM

Tired of all those people leaving church before the end of the service? A simple laser projector at each door sends out a piecing alarm each time the beam is broken. This splendid device will encourage church members to remain dutifully seated until dismissed.

321-B $2,555.09

TWO-DAY CLERGY SHIRT

Designed for the busy pastor or deacon whose schedule won't permit many clothing changes. Reversible design allows for quick change — turning those food stains on the outside to the inside and presenting a fresh-looking replacement. Scotchguarded, this fine shirt resists perspiration.

CC-2   (short sleeve) $45.92
CC-2A   (long sleeve) $52.13

LITURGICAL AEROBICS

Now available from Balmy on videotape: Bench Pressing the 1979 Book of Common Prayer by the Rev. Geoffrey Plabbitt, the Episcopal priest who created the concept of "Liturgical Aerobics." A perfect gift for a pastor who is suffering from overweight and lack of exercise.

2196-DJ $175.99

STAY-LIT ALTAR CANDLES

Provide hours of fun as your pastor watches acolytes attempt to extinguish these candles in vain. Developed by the Ecclesial Gag Company.

1429-WM $56.00 (box)

FOLDING TITANIUM ALTAR FOR ASTROCHAPLAINS

This special corrosion-resistant item comes with mounting brackets and Eucharistic vessels designed for use in zero gravity.

8809-PC $45,886.29

VIBRATOR PULPIT

Created for the pastor with foot and leg problems. Soothing vibrations calm strained muscles and tendons while he/she preaches. Fifteen power settings. Turn up the power for sermon climax.

1968-AQ $12,444.10
                    (installation extra)

VACUUM-TUBE ALMS COLLECTION SYSTEM

Designed to operate like the ones at bank drive-ins. Pew mounted with central receiving station in basement or secured room. Ready to install for 200-pew church. Eliminate the time-consuming offertory!

4715-CL $103,911.43
                    (includes installation)

INFLATABLE CONGREGATION

The invention of the century! This device is absolutely perfect for the small church. Make those pews look FULL! One quick twist of the air valve on our patented "Pneuma Tank," and, presto, you have a pew full of excited-looking people. And, for preaching practice, what a marvelous way to finely hone that scintillating sermon by pretending you have a church full of eager parishioners! One (1) air tank comes with order.

6821-ZO $3,239.56

HEAVENLY SECURITY SYSTEMS

The perfect Christmas gift for your pastor! Protect his/her church from burglary with Balmy's Heavenly Security Systems. If a burglar gains entrance to your sanctuary, traditional devices send out a silent alarm to police. Balmy's system does this — and more!

Once the alarm has been tripped, an infrared scanning device locates, tracks, and photographs the thief. The unit then automatically flips on all the interior lights, and a digitized recording of a 250-member choir singing Handel's Messiah fills the building with over 170 decibels of sound. Optional features include the Avenging Legion of Angels Holographic Companion to the Messiah, and up to 15 minutes of your pastor's favorite sermon. Guaranteed to bring any burglar or vandal to their knees!

3186-HSS $12,995.32

PREACHING GLOVES AND BAPTISMAL GLOVES

Another first for Balmy! Genius is as genius does. Here are preaching gloves for your pastor to wear during the winter when the thermostat gets turned down because of budget cutbacks. Also available are baptismal gloves with rubberized tips so that a child won't squirt out of your pastor's hands.

62QG-58 Preaching gloves $117.57
29PX-49 Baptismal gloves $98.33

BALMY'S ROBOT PASTOR

Japanese Buddhists reportedly have unveiled a "robot priest" which is computer-programmed to perform a variety of rituals. Not to be outdone, Balmy Clergy Supply introduces the Balmy Robot Pastor, which can be used by churches as temporary replacements for vacationing or ill pastors. The Robot Pastor is programmed to deliver any of 487 15-minute sermons, and to scan the congregation and zap with a mild electric shock anyone who falls asleep or fails to put anything in the offering plates. The Robot Pastor also is programmed to identify heretics and church members who have fallen behind on their pledges, and to sound a full-scale trumpet blast when one is identified.

7901-RP $59,467.99

CHURCH FURNISHINGS OF DISTINCTION

Your Bishop sits in splendor and regal comfort on our Mark VIII episcopal throne. Made of rare and rich woods and upholstered with the finest silks, this handsome furniture will adorn your sanctuary with such glorious beauty that, even when your Bishop is absent, it will seem to vibrate with the Bishop's power and grace. You may also wish to consider our Mark IX throne, which has both a built-in vibrator and heat massager if your Bishop is advanced in years.

Make a dramatic homiletical entrance with the Elevating Pulpit. This amazing device is designed to rise up out of the floor with you standing behind it. You will ascend miraculously from the church basement. Imagine the awe-inspiring response from your congregation at this magnificent sight. Comes standard with 1,000 digitized trumpet fanfares to herald your arrival.
For more information and prices, write to Balmy Clergy Supply.

SEEDBED PRESS, INC.
announces the publication of a new six-volume edition of The Young Christian's Illustrated Encyclopedia of Theology. The set contains over 20,000 color plates depicting

heretofore inexplicable theological concepts for young minds. Designed specifically for ages 4 through 12. Now available from Balmy Clergy Supply.
3862-NR $825.95

**TO ALL THOSE PLANNING
A CHRISTMAS TOUR OF THE
HOLY LAND WITH
REV. RALPH PUTMAN**
Pastor Putman has recently been advised that hostilities in some of the areas which the tour will visit make ground travel hazardous. But take heart! Refusing to cancel the tour, Pastor Putman has arranged for six attack helicopters to serve as transport. Unfortunately, the cost to operate the helicopters will increase the cost of the tour by $1,200 per person. Pastor Putman regrets this small inconvenience to faithful pilgrims.

"It's a Wonderful Life must be on."
© 1994 Harley L. Schwadron

THE SCROOGE AWARD

Every year, just before Christmas, the time comes for your local newspaper or TV station to interview the native psychologists and psychiatrists about all the people who get the blues during the Christmas holidays and who, incidentally, need their help, for $100 to $150 an hour, to get through the Christmas season.

The story has become a Christmas tradition in the secular press, almost as predictable as the story of Scrooge. Christians who celebrate Christmas joyfully and hopefully, even though they may be suffering poor health, unemployment or other sorrows, are rarely interviewed.

The board of directors of the Fellowship of Merry Christians, therefore, decided to balance things out by announcing two awards every year at Christmas time: the Scrooge Award and the True Spirit of Christmas Present Award.

FMC's Scrooge Award is given annually "to the organization or group whose humbug most insistently dampens the Spirit of Christmas at Christmas time."

FMC's True Spirit of Christmas Present Award is given annually "to the person or organization who best exemplifies the True Spirit of Christmas Present."

FMC gave its first annual Scrooge Award in 1994 to the Jesus Seminar, a collection of 150 religion scholars, for their *timing* in publishing — at Christmas time, 1993 — a book casting deadly serious doubts about who Jesus is and what He said. The scholars maintained that no more than 18 percent of the sayings attributed to Jesus in the New Testament were actually spoken by Him.

FMC gave its first annual True Spirit of Christmas Present Award to 85-years-young author Sherwood Eliot Wirt for his book, *The Book of Joy*.

FMC gave its 1995 Scrooge Award to the Legal Department and Retail Support Department of the U.S. Postal Service in Washington, D.C., for collaborating on a policy banning the use of decorative signs or messages saying "Merry Christmas" or "Happy Hanukkah" in Post Office lobbies.

The Fellowship urged everyone to protest the ban by greeting all postal clerks and mail carriers with a hearty "Merry Christmas!" and a smile sometime during the Christmas season, and a "Happy Hanukkah!" on December 18, the first day of Hanukkah.

FMC gave its 1995 True Spirit of Christmas Award to David Rupert, acting postmaster in Jackson, Wyoming, and chaplain of the National League of Postmasters, for his relentless efforts to get U.S. Postal Service officials in Washington to lift the ban.

Rupert, a member of Jackson Hole Christian Center in Jackson and an FMC member, inspired the National League of Postmasters to present a petition signed by 280 postmasters throughout the country asking Postmaster General Marvin Runyon to lift or modify the ban.

Rupert also noted that when the Post Office released its new 1995 holiday stamps in October, "for the first year in recent memory, not one of them has the word 'Christmas' on it. This year they're calling them 'holiday traditional stamps.' "

Writing in the *Federal Times*, Ed Winsten suggested a new holiday slogan for postmasters to decorate their lobbies: "It's beginning to look a lot like mid-to-late December."

And writing in *USA Today*, columnist Joe Urschel commented: "Christmas generates enormous business for the Post Office, and it wants you to use its service to deliver your packages and cards. But what is the one word they avoid in this promotional push? Christmas!"

"If I could work my will, every idiot who goes about with 'Merry Christmas' on his lips should be boiled with his own pudding and buried with a stake of holly through his heart."
—Ebenezer Scrooge
A Christmas Carol

"More people, on the whole, are humbugged by believing in nothing than by believing in too much."
—P.T. Barnum

"Should we not see that lines of laughter about the eyes are just as much marks of faith as are the lines of care and seriousness? Is it only earnestness that is baptized? Is laughter pagan? We have already allowed too much that is good to be lost to the church and cast many pearls before swine. A church is in a bad way when it banishes laughter from the sanctuary and leaves it to the cabaret, the nightclub and the toastmasters."

—Helmut Thielicke
via Gary Snavely, West Linn, OR

HOW TO EXPAND CHRISTMAS JOY YEAR 'ROUND

"If joy is our Christian birthright, why are we so lackadaisical in cultivating it?" asks *JN* consulting editor Edward R. Walsh of Westbury, NY. "How can we enlarge our capacity for joy?" Here are Walsh's suggestions:
* Pray daily that the Holy Spirit will bless you with joy.
* Select religious reading that emphasizes joyful aspects of our faith. A diet of doom-and-gloom forced feedings won't elevate your mood.
* Act joyfully, even if your mood is otherwise. And as sure as day follows night, the darkness in your soul will yield to the dawn of a brighter outlook.
* Share your good mood.
* Share joyful news. Joy is contagious. Write upbeat letters. Make upbeat phone calls. Speak well of others in their presence.
* Cultivate friends who share your philosophy. Avoid the nay-sayers, the put-down artists, and people-knockers. Seek out the joy-givers and let them refresh your battered spirit.
* Imagine yourself in joyful company. The people you admire can cheer you up. Do you have heroes or heroines? Stand mentally in their presence, and absorb the joyful glow of their personalities.
* Join the Fellowship of Merry Christians, or make a needy person a Merry Christian.

"The very society of joy redoubles it."
　　　　　　　—Robert South

PILGRIMS' JOURNEY TO CHRISTMAS JOY
"He who gives joy to the world is raised higher among men than he who conquers the world."
　　　　　　　—Richard Wagner

"When I think of God, my heart is so filled with joy that the notes fly off as from a spindle."
　　　　　　　—Joseph Haydn (1809)
　　　　　　　　when criticized for the
　　　　　　　　joyfulness of his music.

"I am always happy. I, who deserve the severest discipline, feel joys so continual and so great that I can scarce contain them."
　　　　　　　—Brother Lawrence
　　　　　　　The Practice of the Presence of God

"He who is truly a lover of Jesus Christ does not say his prayers like other men, for seated in his right mind and ravished with Christ's love above himself, he is taken into a marvelous mirth!"
　　　　　　　—Richard Rolle
　　　　　　　English writer (1349)

"The most manifest sign of wisdom is continued cheerfulness."
　　　　　　　—Montaigne

"Find joy in everything that leads to God."
　　　　　　　—Teresa of Avila

"The soul of one who serves God always swims in joy, always keeps holiday, and is always in the mood for singing."
　　　　　　　—John of the Cross
　　　　　　　(1591 A.D.)

"A Christian as such (according to the design of his Religion, and in proportion to his compliance with its dictates) is the most jocund and blithe person in the world; always in humor and full of cheer."
—Isaac Barrow (1686)

"It is possible to live for the next life and be merry in this."
—Thomas More

"Man is for joy and joy is for man. I think joy is not joy at all unless it is in man's possession. The human heart is so dependent upon joy that, without joy, it cannot find rest. Joy is true joy only in so far as it is possessed by the heart of man.
"Humor is the foundation of reconciliation."
—Francis de Sales

"The way to cheerfulness is to keep our bodies in exercise and our minds at ease."
—Richard Steele (1729)

"It is God's will not merely that we should be happy, but that we should make ourselves happy. This is true morality."
—Immanuel Kant

"It is the heart that is not sure of its God that is afraid to laugh in His presence."
—George MacDonald

"In laughter, man's freedom becomes manifest."
—Friedrich Duerrenmatt

"A person without a sense of humor is like a wagon without springs, jolted by every pebble in the road."
—Henry Ward Beecher

"Cana of Galilee... Ah, that sweet miracle! It was not men's grief, but their joy Christ visited. He worked His first miracle to help men's gladness."
—Feodor Dostoevsky

"The true test of religion — does it make wings to lift someone up, or is it a deadweight to drag them down? Does it make it a joy or a depression? Are people haunted or helped? Does it carry you or do you have to carry it?"
—William Barclay

"How necessary it is to cultivate a spirit of joy. To act lovingly is to begin to feel loving, and certainly to act joyfully brings joy to others, which in turn makes one feel joyful. I believe we are called to the duty of delight."
—Dorothy Day

"I think we all sin by needlessly disobeying the apostolic injunction to 'rejoice' as much as by anything else."
—C.S. Lewis
The Problem of Pain

"Sin causes the cup of joy to spring a leak."
—via Rev. Robert E. Harris
Asheville, NC

"Joy is the holy fire that keeps our purpose warm and our intelligence aglow."
—Helen Keller

"Christianity is a strangely cheery religion. It knows the world wants to pitch itself into hell, is always in the act of doing just that. But it also knows that nothing but an adamantine will can separate us from the love of Christ."
—Flannery O'Connor

"Walk cheerfully over the world. Sing and rejoice, Children of the Day and of the Light..."
—George Fox (1624-91)

"You pray in your distress and in your need; would that you might pray also in the fullness of your joy and in your days of abundance."
—Kahlil Gibran

"Don't forget. God loves you."
© 1995 Ed Sullivan

"When you toss out the Christmas tree, be careful you don't throw out the Christmas spirit with it."
—via Rev. Felix A. Lorenz, Jr.
Northville, MI

"We wish you a Merry Christmas and a Happy New You."
—3-year-old Luke Samra's
version of a Christmas carol

"I bring you news of great joy!"
—Luke 2:10

A CHRISTMAS PRAYER FOR A JOYFUL HEART

"As we celebrate the joyful feast of Christmas, and look at the crib scene, we should reflect on the fact that we best communicate with babies by a smile. We so often pray to God for a 'clean heart.' Why not ask for a 'joyful heart' this Christmas?"
—Rev. Julian Davies
The Cord

~ 𝒞hapter 13 ~
𝒯estimonials

The healing power of holy humor

"Thank you for waiting such a long time. You have the
patience of Job, Mr....er...Job."

© 1995 Harley L. Schwadron

On his popular Sunday-night program "Amplify" on Radio Station KDKA, Pittsburgh, Rev. Ron Lengwin was interviewing *JN* editor Cal Samra on his book *The Joyful Christ: The Healing Power of Humor* when a listener called in this story:

There used to be a popular restaurant in Pittsburgh called Captain Cook's. The owner, Barney Cook, was a real clown and cut-up. He was always playing practical jokes, and cheering everybody up. Barney had a loudspeaker and would announce every customer's name as they came in.

One day, one of Barney's friends, Joe the mailman, came by, and while he was eating dinner, he suddenly slumped over on the floor. Joe's face turned blue, and he was gasping for breath, like he was having a heart attack.

Everybody panicked. People were running around calling for a doctor, a nurse, an ambulance. Barney calmly told everyone to move aside. He got down on his hands and knees, and whispered in the man's ear: "Joe, can you hear me?"

"Yeah, I can hear you," Joe replied weakly.

"Have you paid your check?" Barney asked.

Joe started laughing — and laughing and laughing. A healthy color returned to his face, and by the time the ambulance arrived, Joe was up and assuring everyone he was feeling fine.

HUMOR IS THE BEST MEDICINE

JN consulting editor Donald L. Cooper, M.D., is team physician for the football and basketball teams and director of the Student Health Center at Oklahoma State University. He was appointed by President Reagan to the President's Council on Physical Fitness and Sports, and reappointed by President Bush. He is also a popular speaker and humorist.

Dr. Cooper, a Presbyterian layman, became a humorist many years ago after a couple of crippling episodes with depression. One episode hospitalized him and brought him to the edge of suicide.

He says that his faith, humor, the love and support of his family, exercise, and medication prescribed by a physician helped him ride out both episodes of depression.

He advises depressed persons to "hang on to your faith" and "cultivate a sense of humor." He says: "Don't give up. Depression is self-limited, and if you hang on, it will pass."

Says Dr. Cooper: "I give 30 to 40 lectures a year on stress management, and my No. 1 emphasis on managing stress is laughter."

Dr. Cooper tells jokes and stories endlessly. He observes that the great medical missionary and Nobel Prize winner, Albert Schweitzer, had a keen sense of humor and often told jokes and stories to cheer up his patients.

CONFESSIONS OF HUNTER ("PATCH") ADAMS, M.D.

FMC member "Patch" Adams, M.D., says that years ago, when he was a physician in Washington, D.C., he was so deadly serious about everything that he once tried to kill himself, and committed himself to a mental hospital.

There, he says, "I grew to respect what matters in life: wonder and curiosity and love and faith and family and friends and nature and humor."

Dr. Adams, adding another dimension to his medical practice, became a clown and humorist. He is now a popular speaker on campuses and before medical organizations, and is known as "the clown-prince of physicians." He also organized the Gesundheit Institute in Arlington, VA, with the aim of establishing a community of health professionals and patients "glued together by fun."

"Fun," he says, "has overwhelming medicinal effects on our patients. So many fewer pain medications! I am amazed at how humor has had a beneficial impact on disease, especially chronic disease such as arthritis and mental illness. Humor has healing power. Today, hospitals are places of seriousness and solemnity. There is no healing power in seriousness and solemnity."

Dr. Adams and his associates use zany humor and clowning along with their medical treatments and prescriptions. They do outrageously funny things to get patients to laugh.

Adams once dressed up in a white robe with angel's wings and went into a depressed patient's room and loudly proclaimed: "Coming attractions!"

He also uses humor to attack the despair of potential suicides. "Many a suicide call to my office has begun with, 'Doctor, I want to kill myself.' I just answer: 'Your place or mine?' The callers laugh, and I invite them over to talk." Adams says getting a suicidal person to laugh often can be a turning point.

"When a person says, 'That doctor has a good bedside manner,' what are they really talking about? The elements of love and humor the doctor brings into the room," says Adams.

He tells his audiences: "The most revolutionary act you can do in today's world is to be publicly happy."

"A smile across the aisle of a bus in the morning could save a suicide later in the day."
—Archbishop Fulton J. Sheen

"Show me a patient who is able to laugh and play, who enjoys living, and I'll show you someone who is going to live longer. Laughter makes the unbearable bearable and a patient with a well developed sense of humor has a better chance of recovery than a stolid individual who seldom laughs."
—Bernie Siegel, M.D.

"Our medical benefits are second to none; we pray for your health every day."
© 1995 M. Larry Zanco

"Laughter is internal jogging. We have a lot of evidence that shows mirth and laughter affect most of the

major physical systems of the body in a positive way. You
can laugh a lot more times a day than you can do pushups."
                    —William Fry, M.D.
                    Stanford University Medical
                    School

"When you laugh, the whole system vibrates, a dancing
diaphragm, dancing cells. All the cells are happy, and when
you are happy, you have a longer life. If you don't furnish
your cells with this vibration of dancing, which we call
laughing, you are robbing them of life. Laughter is a
transformer."
                    —Samuel Avital
                    Sabbath Time
                    via Rev. Felix A. Lorenz, Jr.

"A prominent doctor discovered that cheerful people resist
disease better than chronic grumblers. He concluded that the
surly bird gets the germ."
                    —Lorin D. Whittaker, M.D.
                    Laugh Away Your Tensions

"Some early American Indians designated tribal clowns to
work the group on ceremonial occasions. Medicine men
knew that humor heals, so most of the clowns were doctors,
and most of the doctors were clowns."
                    —*York (PA) Dispatch*
                    via Rev. Bob Anderson

"Health and cheerfulness mutually beget each other.
Laughter breaks the gloom which depresses the mind and
dampens the spirit."
                    —Thomas Addison, M.D.
                    English physician (1793-1860)

"One of the holiest women I have ever known did little
with her life in terms of worldly success; her gift was that of
bringing laughter with her, no matter how dark or grievous

the occasion. Wherever she was, holy laughter was present to heal and redeem."

—Madeleine L'Engle

"Medicine consists of amusing the patient while nature cures the disease."

—Voltaire

THE FAMILY CIRCUS

" ...and give us our trespasses as we give it
to those who trespass against us..."
Reprinted with permission of Bil Keane

"We have a support group here at our church's Family Practice & Counseling Center, and we always open our sessions with a tidbit or two from *JN*. It really helps these persons suffering from cancer, MS, chronic depression, and a variety of other illnesses.

"Several years ago, I began giving a talk which my wife entitled, 'Take Two Laughs and Call Me in the Morning.' Since my ministry is in our health center, I get a chance to do my stand-up comedy stuff, then help participants understand the therapy of humor."

—Rev. Barron B. Maberry
St. Matthew's Evangelical
Lutheran Church
Washington, DC

"I was at a hospital in Lorain, OH, and met a sad man who was a patient there. I had some time so we talked for 90 minutes. I told him many of the jokes and stories in *JN*. He was elated. His wife and daughter came in, so I left and said I would be back later. When I returned, his daughter hugged me for 'doing what I did for her father.' What a reward!"

—Otto G. Lucius
Avon Lake, OH

"I shared *The Joyful Noiseletter's* jokes recently with a friend who was facing serious cancer surgery. Needless to say, there was a great deal of prayer, too. You can imagine our elation when the doctor made the incision and the expected cancer was gone! Extensive tests had shown the cancer to be there. Your ministry of humor helped us all in the midst of this, and we are very thankful."

—Jean W. Spencer
Camarillo, CA

"During my father's 18-month battle with cancer, his subscription to *JN* was a great boost to his morale. The uplifting comments and humorous insights helped to provide a refreshing interlude."

—Rev. Bill Pyatt
First United Methodist Church
Carterville, IL

"I am a member of a Humor Focus Group at the hospital where I work. We have found that there is a distinct correlation between humor and health. We also believe that a sound spiritual belief system is important in physical, emotional and psychological health. As a member of the health profession for 15 years, I have seen the healing power that humor and a strong spiritual belief system have. Combining these two ideas can only double the healing effects."

—Bonnie Graboski
Allentown, PA

"I wholeheartedly agree that Christianity should be joyful. Two years ago we lost a beautiful son to suicide. I have relied heavily on the Lord and humor to recover from this great loss."
—Nancy Newkom
Yuba City, CA

"I work extensively with senior citizen shut-ins. We have great hilarity and much laughter. Those with a joyful heart are so much more able to cope with their infirmities and bounce back after lapses of illness."
—Mrs. Regina L. Kleekamp
Bonne Terre, MO

"If people could laugh 15 times a day, there would be fewer doctor bills."
—Dr. Joel Goodman
Director, The Humor Project
Saratoga Springs, NY

"I look forward to receiving *JN* each month. As a person who suffered from fits of deep depression for years, it is so encouraging for me to find that there is such a thing as a Merry Christian, and with God's help I am becoming one. It's so much more fun and a much better life-style. I thank you and I thank God for you."
—Bonnie Habbersett
Livonia, MI

"Living with a chronic illness has its drawbacks, but a liberal sprinkling of chuckles and jokes from *JN* helps everyone cope with the roller coaster of everyday living."
—Dolores O'Leary
Puyallup, WA

Fr. Alfred Stangl, a St. Cloud Hospital chaplain, claims that laughter can be therapeutic.
"I remember one evening I visited a woman who was

suffering from deep depression, to give her communion. But she was in the middle of a shower, so instead of drying her off, the nurse helped her slip her robe on. But first, so that the robe wouldn't get soaked, she draped her with newspapers.

"After I left and she resumed her shower, the imprint of the *St. Cloud Times* color comic section was all over her body like a tattoo. She and the nurse laughed so hard that she was discharged the next day, her depression as passé as yesterday's news."

—via Joseph Young
St. Cloud (MN) Visitor

"Reading the book *The Joyful Christ* by Cal Samra several years ago was part of a breakthrough experience for me, as I was taking clinical pastoral education in preparation for my vocational transition into hospital chaplaincy. I am currently Protestant chaplain at St. Bernardine Medical Center in San Bernadino, CA, and I have found great satisfaction in incorporating the healing energy of humor into my ministry.

"In my ministry to a patient in our psychiatric unit, I utilized the picture by Frances Hook on page 174 of the book entitled 'My Friend,' depicting a smiling Christ tenderly holding a young girl. Since the patient had had an extremely abusive father, this picture had enormous impact on her in helping her to see God as truly loving, not angry or punishing. No other picture captures the pure delight and love on Jesus' face as he holds the little girl.

"May God continue to bless your healing ministry."

—Chaplain Robert W. Engstrom
San Bernadino, CA

Terry Anderson, the former chief Middle East correspondent for the Associated Press, says his Catholic faith and his sense of humor "kept me from giving in to despair" during the 6 $^1/_2$ dark years he was held by pro-Iranian kidnappers in Lebanon.

Shortly after he returned to the States in 1992, Anderson wrote to the editor of *JN*: "I agree wholeheartedly that laughter and joy should be a major — perhaps the largest — part of being a Christian. The Fellowship of Merry Christians sounds like a great and useful group. God bless you and all the members."

'SHE THINKS SHE'S A WITCH!'

The late Baptist pastor Tal D. Bonham was one of the best humorists in the Protestant world. Bonham, who was then executive director of the State Convention of Baptists in Ohio, was an early supporter of FMC and a consulting editor to *JN*. At an FMC playshop in Indianapolis in 1987, he had people almost rolling in the aisles with his jokes and stories.

Bonham told a story about his wife Faye's year-long battle with depression, ending in hospitalization. Various treatments had failed to dissipate the depression.

When Bonham was driving her home from the hospital after discharge, she looked into the mirror and said: "I look like a witch."

"No, you don't," Bonham said. But then he suggested that the Bonhams play a practical joke on Faye's friends.

When her friends called to inquire about her, Bonham carefully explained that Faye was feeling better, but she had occasional episodes when she thinks she's a witch, and would get a broom and ride around the house.

One friend shouted into the phone: "She thinks she's a witch!"

"The spell doesn't last long," Bonham explained. "When you come, just stay calm and act as if nothing is happening."

When Faye's friends came to the Bonham house one night, bringing food, Faye mounted the broom and galloped around the house. Her friends tried to act as if everything was normal and chatted about other things while Faye was cavorting around the house.

When the Bonhams finally let their friends in on their practical joke, everyone, including Faye, laughed hysterically.

It was then that Bonham decided to put together a book of clean jokes. He asked Faye to help him with the book, and the depression dissipated as she worked on the book and cultivated her sense of humor. The book, *The Treasury of Clean Church Jokes*, was one of several clean joke books by Bonham that were published by Broadman & Holman, Nashville, TN.

'J'ARMING FOR THE HEALTH OF IT'

Some people believe they can face aches, pains, depression, tension or anger only with the help of pills and drugs. Medication can help, but Dr. Dale L. Anderson also believes in stimulating the divinely created "internal pharmacy" in your head.

The Roseville, MN, physician, an FMC member, touts the body's production of endorphins, chemicals he calls "inner uppers" that help make us healthy and "high on life." Dr. Anderson believes that laughter is among the best ways to produce these pharmaceutical marvels, along with faith, exercise, singing and positive mental images.

To get the body to release endorphins, Dr. Anderson has invented an enjoyable method he calls "J'ARMing" — jogging with the arms. He has demonstrated this physical activity, which resembles conducting an orchestra with the wave of a baton, to thousands of patients and workshop participants.

He has produced a book and a cassette about "J'ARMing." His wife calls him "Prince J'ARMing."

Persons who "J'ARM" can use chopsticks, forks, pencils, or other assorted objects to conduct.

"J'ARMing" improves the flow of blood to the brain, produces more endorphins, and strengthens immune systems. "Laughter truly is the best medicine," he says.

He adds: "The good feelings which we Christians get from prayer, belief, hope, love, joy, etc. are undoubtedly the result of divinely created chemicals which these positive feelings produce in our bodies. Religion and following Christian teachings are ways to raise these beneficial chemicals."

For his patients and audiences, the doctor often orders "a fake laughter prescription" consisting of standing before a mirror for 15 seconds twice a day and enjoying a hearty belly laugh.

Dr. Anderson suggests that persons everywhere should "attack life with silliness." He makes sure that people attending his seminars sing silly songs with him. "I'm not offering a panacea," Dr. Anderson says, "but health education should be a lot more exciting than it has been. It should be health entertainment."

Dr. Anderson is a member of the United Church of Christ in Falcon Heights, MN.

JN consulting editor Barbara Shlemon Ryan of Brea, CA, is a registered nurse who is the author of *Healing Prayer* and *To Heal as Jesus Healed,* two splendid books on the healing power of prayer. Barbara also has been the administrator of the Association of Christian Therapists (A.C.T.), an organization of physicians, nurses, counselors, and clergy who strive to integrate their faith experience with their practice.

"Laughter among members of the helping professions is a safety valve to release the tensions which build up inside as we encounter suffering, sickness, and death," Barbara says. "During our yearly A.C.T. conferences, we regularly schedule an evening of fun to remind ourselves of the importance of laughter in bringing balance into our lives.

"I vividly remember one party when we blew up balloons, filled them with water, and threw them at one another. We were all soaked to the skin and aching from laughter. I discovered one of

"Let us join in silent prayer. Please turn off your beepers."
© 1992 Goddard Sherman

the physicians, a very prominent oncologist, sitting on the floor with tears streaming down his face.

"'These are tears of joy,' he told me. 'My childhood was very rigid and I was never allowed to have a birthday party with balloons and silly games. Tonight made up for a lot of empty years.' "

Adds Barbara: "The secret of survival in Christian service is to develop a sense of humor that can gladden our heart and offset the burdens we sometimes must carry."

In March, 1991, FMC member Antoinette Bosco, a columnist for Catholic News Service and executive director of the *Litchfield (CT) Times*, contributed a front-page article to *JN* under the headline, "The saints were not sad sacks."

"The saints," she wrote, "were so full of joy that even pain and martyrdom could not destroy their sense of humor." Since then, Toni Bosco has been assailed by a succession of devastating tragedies. Her 27-year-old son, suffering from deep depression, shot himself. Then she received the horrifying news that another son, 41, and his wife had been murdered in their bed by an armed intruder in their Bigfork, MT, home.

Bosco wrote a tender and inspiring book about her struggles to cope with these tragedies. *The Pummeled Heart: Finding Peace through Pain* is an affirmation of faith in the midst of torment.

Keep your faith and keep your sense of humor, she advises. "If you want to gain strength after being broken, it'll never happen without a sense of humor. Laughter is still the greatest medicine. If any of you need encouragement, you should get in touch with the Fellowship of Merry Christians and the wonderful tidbits in *The Joyful Noiseletter*."

God, Bosco says, gives us both the healing gift of tears and the healing gift of laughter.

FMC member Joan Burney, a counselor and journalist in Hartington, NE, wrote:

"The more I read the Bible, the more it seemed to me that Christians should be the most joyful people in the whole world. So why aren't we? Why the dour face and woeful expectations? I asked myself, looking into the mirror. Though I desired it, and prayed for it, my metamorphosis from a frightened Christian into a joyful one seemed to be slow in coming.

"Some weeks ago, I began to metamorphose in joyful leaps. A friend sent me a picture of 'Jesus Laughing' by Willis Wheatley. And there it was. The mental picture which had been eluding me. Another friend told me about the Fellowship of Merry Christians, and I joined.

"We should allow the merriment of Christ to seep into our souls."

"Laugh and the world laughs with you. Cry and you simply get wet," says FMC member Cliff Thomas, R.Ph., "the Philosophical Pharmacist" from Belle Fourche, SD.

Humorist Thomas estimates he has dispensed one million prescriptions in his 38 years as a pharmacist. He charged for the pills, but threw the humor and philosophy in free. It was a toss-up, he says, as to which did the customers the most good.

Thomas, a popular speaker, says: "I have found that ownership of humor lasts about 10 minutes. Most humorists steal a lot. The first time I use someone else's joke, I say, 'As Bill Cosby said…' Next time, it's 'As I once heard another speaker say…' The third time, it's 'As I've always said…' "

Thomas' motto: "Let's make this a laughing world. If you meet someone who doesn't have a smile, give them one of yours."

FMC member Lila Green, author of *Making Sense of Humor* and a lecturer and consultant on humor in health care at the University of Michigan in Ann Arbor, MI, says that humor is helpful to all kinds of patients, including geriatrics and Alzheimers' patients. She applauds hospitals who have established "humor rooms" for patients, and urges physicians and other health care professionals to use "humor prescriptions."

FMC member Leslie Gibson, RN, of Dunedin, FL, has pioneered in the establishment of "comedy carts" for patients at hospitals in Florida.

FMC member Mark Therrien, a Wisconsin psychologist, has been putting on seminars called "The Power of Positive Insanity."

He believes people take illness too seriously. "My wife's grandmother had cancer and was in terrible shape," he says. "We brought her flowers and one of those arrows you can wear on your head. Then we had an unusual family photo taken. We were all wearing five-inch banana noses.

"Grandma just cracked up. She laughed and laughed. We're so serious around the terminally ill, but people are capable of joy up until they take their last breath. That's why clowns are so effective in hospitals. If humor is used correctly, it can be a real healing force."

"A clown is a poet in action. He can show us how to laugh at ourselves because his own laughter was born of tears. The clown has confronted sorrow and suffering and pain, and transformed them into compassion. Clowns are healers, and the world has never needed them more than it does now."

—Sr. Marie-Celeste Fadden, OCD
Clowns and Children of the World
Reno, NV

"It was a wonderful experience for St. Stephen's Episcopal Church to sponsor an FMC playshop. The playshop leaders, Ed and Marji Elzey ("Marji and Roma") exude a blessed radiance of joy that is unmistakably Christ at work. With FMC's marvelous materials and PR support, it was a fantastic part of our parish life. People already have been asking what's next, and when they can come back. A sense of revival has hit our parish, and joy is still bursting forth. Thank you for giving us this blessing. I

love your idea of a House of Laughter. Please keep working on it."
> —Lynn Herne
> St. Stephen's Episcopal Church
> New Hartford, NY

"FMC's retreat at Alverna in Indianapolis was just what the doctor ordered! I feel I got rid of a lot of the stress I was feeling prior to the retreat. It does me so much good to have those belly laughs, and just to let it rip!"
> —Sr. Helene Schneider
> Highland, IL

FMC member William W. Travis of Birmingham, AL, a freelance writer and speaker, begins his talks on laughter with Psalm 23:3 — "He restoreth my soul" — because, he says, "I believe God's favorite tool for restoring souls is laughter."

"The joy that comes from God is part of the Christian's armor. Sin insinuates itself more easily into a downcast heart than into a joyous spirit. Germs carrying disease infect most easily a body debilitated by despondency. So do the termites of the spirit. They enter without ceremony and eat away the health of the soul.

"I know many in the lay ministry of our church who are joyful and large-hearted, to whom people have gone with sad countenances and heavy hearts, only to return with joy showing all over their faces. They go in looking pale and come out flushed with excitement. They meet with joy! This is the mark of the Holy Spirit."
> —Selwyn Hughes
> *Every Day with Jesus*

"I work in a health food store and have a 'Healthy Bulletin Board' for jokes and cartoons. Sometimes I believe the joke board does more good than anything on the shelves."
> —Armida Baldwin
> Shawnee Mission, KS

Even the Hemlock Society, promoters of euthanasia, has become interested in therapeutic humor.

News item from the *Nashville Tennessean:* "Humor and its therapeutic effect on personal health is the subject of an address to be delivered by Perry H. Biddle Jr. at 7 p.m. Feb. 16 at the Hemlock of Tennessee chapter at the Unitarian Universalist Church."

—via George Goldtrap
Madison, TN

THE JOYFUL GOSPEL OF A FAITH-FILLED PHYSICIAN

The Gospel with the strongest emphasis on joy was written by a faith-filled physician with a keen sense of humor. Luke's Gospel is brimming with joy, irony, humor, and comic reversal.

It is Luke who quotes Jesus as saying: "Blessed are you who weep now, for you shall laugh." (Luke 6:21)

It is Luke ("the beloved physician," as Paul called him) who carefully records Jesus' and the apostles' many healing miracles — and the great joy surrounding them — in his Gospel and in the Acts of the Apostles.

FMC member Joseph A. Grassi, a professor of religious studies at Santa Clara University, makes these observations in a captivating book titled *God Makes Me Laugh: A New Approach to Luke.*

Grassi notes that "there are signs that 'the quest for the historical Jesus' has come to a near impasse despite the work of great scholars of the past 40 years." In Luke's writings, on the other hand, Grassi finds "a comic eschatology — comic in the sense that God acts in surprising and unusual ways that make people jump with joy and laugh."

"Jesus was not a circus clown; he was not an entertainer, or a trickster," Grassi says. "However, his actions and teaching style were a striking humorous contrast to the serious conventional piety of his time."

The difference between Jesus and the stern, ascetic John the Baptist "was like that between a dirge and a dance," says Grassi.

Luke's Gospel also focuses on the paradoxical contrast between Jesus and the Pharisees, Grassi says, because he wanted to show that religion should be "a wedding feast for all with a happy bridegroom leading the festivities," not a legalistic organization presided over by dour teachers.

Luke's Gospel, the author says, also is full of comic reversals in which the "included" become the excluded; the "excluded," the included; the "unclean" become the clean and the "clean," the unclean.

The leper is touched by Jesus and becomes clean. The Pharisee, who presents himself as clean on the outside, is shown to be unclean on the inside.

There is comic reversal in the parable of the Good Samaritan, and in the parable of the Pharisee and the publican. The proud, self-righteous Pharisee is rejected by God, but the sinful, contrite publican wins God's approval.

"I believe...that dreams are more powerful than facts, that hope always triumphs over experience, that laughter is the only cure for grief, and I believe that love is stronger than death."
—Robert Fulghum
*All I Really Need to Know
I learned in Kindergarten*

"How do you spell 'relief'? L-A-U-G-H!"
—Rev. Dennis O. Rinehart
Warren, OH

"You know you sometimes think yourself into unhappiness, into a depression. Do you know that you can also think yourself into gladness? It is by such thinking that you get well, that you prosper, that your prayers are always answered."
—Albert E. Cliffe

"Humor might be the soul of wellness."
—Dr. Donald B. Ardell

"Strange, when you come to think of it, that of all the countless folk who have lived before our time on this planet, not one is known in history or in legend as having died of laughter."

—Max Beerbohm
via Rev. Roger Wenz
Canton, IL

"The best of healers is good cheer."
—Pindar

"It is requisite for the relaxation of the mind that we make use, from time to time, of playful deeds and jokes..."
—Thomas Aquinas
Summa Theologica

"Jesus is the one who helped me smile, not because of my disability, but in spite of my disability."
—Joni Eareckson Tada

"Have you done something to warrant a drive-by prayer group?"

© 1993 Ed Sullivan

"A good laugh and a long sleep are the two best cures."
—Irish proverb

"The saint is hilarious when he is crushed with difficulties because the thing is so ludicrously impossible to anyone but God."

—Oswald Chambers
My Utmost for His Highest
via William Schuler, M.D.
Mendota, IL

"To be dejected is natural; but to be overcome by dejection is madness and folly. Grieve and weep; but give not way to despondency, nor indulge in complaints. Give thanks to God."
—John Chrysostom (407 A.D.)

"Wondrous is the strength of cheerfulness, and its power of endurance. The cheerful man will do more in the same time, will do it better, will persevere in it longer, than the sad or sullen."

—Thomas Carlyle

"Christian men are but men. They may have a bad liver or an attack of bile, or some trial, and then they get depressed if they have ever so much grace. But what then? Well, then you can get joy and peace through believing. I am the subject of depressions of spirit so fearful that I hope none of you ever gets to such extremes of wretchedness as I go to. But I always get back again by this: I know I trust Christ. I have no reliance but in Him. Because He lives, I shall live also, and I spring to my legs again and fight with my depressions of spirit and my downcast soul and get the victory through it. So may you do, and so you must, for there is no other way of escaping from it. In your most depressed seasons, you are to get joy and peace through believing."
—Charles Spurgeon
19th-century English Baptist
pastor

"It is significant, I think, that Jesus, in dealing with the mentally afflicted, for whom He always showed a particular concern, restored them to sanity by getting rid of their demonic alter ego, thereby making them one person again and delivering them from images. Jesus, the supreme antidote to fantasy and master of reality, as it were, extricated them from the television screen and brought them back into life."

—Malcolm Muggeridge
Christ and the Media

"The relationship of the joy of salvation to improved physical health is a field that needs to be explored in depth. People who have the joy of the Lord in their hearts tend to look different. When joy comes into our lives, we not only feel better and look better, we act better. One thing is certain: Jesus Christ still heals, and whether the healing comes to the Christian through medication, or divine intervention in natural processes, or through the saving balm of joy, it is all from His gracious hand."

—Sherwood Eliot Wirt
The Book of Joy

"I remember an old Arab in North Africa. He gave me mint tea in a glass so coated with use that it was opaque, but he handed me companionship, and the tea was wonderful because of it... I began to formulate a new law regarding despondency. A sad soul can kill you quicker, far quicker, than a germ."

—John Steinbeck
Travels with Charley

THE HEALING POWER OF CELEBRATION

FMC member Marilyn Hood, a member of the Sondancers, a clown troupe in Villa Grove, IL, that uses mime, song, dance, and narration to tell Christ-centered parables, wrote:

"When we worship and celebrate joyfully, we release powerful healing forces within ourselves. When a person consciously sets aside burdens or pains in order to celebrate, he or she is saying, in effect, that God's life is far more important than any problems that they are struggling with.

"As Christians become open to regular, joy-filled celebration, they will find that they are beginning to experience a transformation in attitude. Through celebration, the Christian can participate more fully in the resurrection of Christ, who is the dance at the heart of all things."

"Yes, there is healing power in humor," Lois H. Morgan of Mocksville, NC, wrote *JN*. She sent the following poem which, she said, she wrote "after a very dark depression."

> *Jesus,*
> *I believe you laughed*
> *As Mary bathed you*
> *And Joseph tickled your toes.*
> *I believe you giggled*
> *As you and other children*
> *Played your childhood games.*
> *And when you went*
> *To the Temple*
> *And astounded the teachers,*
> *I believe you chuckled*
> *As all children chuckle*
> *When they stump adults.*
> *And surely there were*
> *Moments of merriment*
> *As you and your disciples*
> *Deepen your relationship.*
> *And as you and Mary*
> *And Martha and Lazarus*
> *Fellowshiped, mirth*
> *Must have been mirrored*
> *On your faces.*
> *Jesus,*

I know you wept
And anguished. But
I believe you laughed, too.
Create in me
The life of laughter.

"They shall obtain joy and gladness, and sorrow and sighing shall flee away."
—Isaiah 35:10

A HEALING PRAYER

"I advise depressed people to pray this simple prayer:
'The joy of the Lord is my strength.' (Nehemiah 8:9-10)
Pray it slowly. Experience the prayer. Let the prayer
become part of you — morning, noon, and night. When
a mood of depression comes upon you, pray it all the
more. I've seen the spirit of depression vanish from many
people when they prayed this prayer continually."
—Rev. George DePrizio
Are You Laughing with Me, Jesus?

About the Authors

Cal Samra is a former newspaper and wire-service reporter. He worked for the *New York Herald Tribune*, the *Newark Evening News, Associated Press, The Ann Arbor News* and *The Battle Creek Enquirer*. He is the former executive director of a psychiatric research foundation, and the author of the best seller: *The Joyful Christ: The Healing Power of Humor*, which sold more than 50,000 copies.

Rose Samra has been involved in music and intercession ministries. She has worked for Christian education, health and agricultural organizations. She is co-author with Cal of *Holy Hilarity: Playshop Guidebook of the Fellowship of Merry Christians.*

The Samras are the parents of three sons, Luke, Matthew and Paul, and live in Portage, Michigan.